MW00744450

PORTRAITS OF MY DAD

PORTRAITS OF MY DAD

Thomas J. Petz

Faithful Editions, LLC
2016

© 2015 Thomas J. Petz
All rights reserved

Unless otherwise noted, scripture quotations are taken from:
THE HOLY BIBLE, NEW INTERNATIONAL VERSION®, NIV® Copyright © 1973, 1978,
1984, 2011 by Biblica, Inc.® Used by permission. All rights reserved worldwide.

Scripture quotations marked (NLT) are taken from the Holy Bible, New Living Translation,
copyright © 1996, 2004, 2007 by Tyndale House Foundation. Used by permission of Tyndale
House Publishers, Inc., Carol Stream, Illinois 60188. All rights reserved.

Printed in the United States of America

This book is dedicated to my mom, whose wit, wisdom, and incredible heart show us on a daily basis how lucky Dad was.

Love each other with genuine affection, and take delight in honoring each other. Never be lazy, but work hard and serve the Lord enthusiastically. Rejoice in our confident hope. Be patient in trouble, and keep on praying. When God's people are in need, be ready to help them. Always be eager to practice hospitality.

Bless those who persecute you. Don't curse them; pray that God will bless them. Be happy with those who are happy, and weep with those who weep. Live in harmony with each other. Don't be too proud to enjoy the company of ordinary people. And don't think you know it all!

Never pay back evil with more evil. Do things in such a way that everyone can see you are honorable. Do all that you can to live in peace with everyone.

Romans 12:10-18 (NLT)

Table of Contents

Preface

LOSING a parent is hard, no matter how old you are. It forces you to examine what you believe about God, the relationship you had with the parent, and the direction your own life is taking. Life can never be the same.

When Dad passed away on October 19, 2014, the rest of my family and I were forced to deal with this very reality. Everyone handles it in a different way—some turn to old letters or mementos for comfort. Some need counseling to process the overwhelming feelings they have. Some turn to the church for insight. For me, someone who needs to have space to just think on and process through things for a while, well, the book you are holding in your hands became how I ended up working through it.

You see, after Dad died, I began to notice how sharing tales and memories about his life brought a strong sense of hope to those who were struggling to deal with his loss. Unexpectedly, many even told me how learning about Dad had helped them to cope with some other pain in their lives they hadn't fully worked through yet. The more I thought about this phenomenon, the more I began to feel a heavy conviction that the things we shared around the time of Dad's passing should be written down so they were not forgotten. Perhaps, by collecting these stories together in one place, they could become something more, a way to honor Dad's legacy in some way.

The problem, I soon discovered, in writing the stories down was that they required a lot of setup and context in order for them to be relatable and understandable. When I started this project, my tendency was to try and convey everything in the context of a much larger narrative that provided the necessary background information for each of the stories that I thought were worth telling. However, I found that by doing so, I was significantly diluting the impact of each story, which was something I did not want. Imagine writing something where you have to remember in excruciating detail things that happened in chapter one in order to understand something that happened much later in the book. It's too distracting and too hard to follow to have flip back and forth between pages of the book all of the time.

It took a while, but I finally discovered a solution for this problem. I decided to treat each story as its own thread with the details needed to understand it in a self-contained package. This ended up working much better, but I struggled with the notion of calling each story a "chapter" in the traditional sense of the word. After some consideration, I decided that the word "portrait" was more appropriate, with each portrait providing a unique perspective or look at the person of Dad. A further advantage of this approach was that it provided greater freedom to the reader to determine their individual reaction to each story, which seemed more appropriate given that when these tales were first told, everyone had a different reaction to them.

With the basic structure figured out, it was then time to get to work. But, as I began to write, I noticed something that I felt needed addressing up front. What I realized was that if this book was something I'd read only a handful of years ago, there are many things that I would have dismissed as exaggeration, coincidence, superstition, or outright lies.

Realizing this about myself (someone who experienced the things you'll read in this book first hand) compelled me to share a few words acknowledging that there may be times while reading this book where you, the reader, may run into something that makes you say something like "I'm not sure I can believe that." For instance, the notion that God still speaks to people was new to me when I was exposed to it just a few years ago, despite having been raised in the church my whole life. That God is always good and is constantly working everything out for those who love Him also seems hard to believe in light of the events we see unfolding in the news and some of the things you read in the Old Testament.

My intention in writing this book is not to engage in a debate about the veracity of these sometimes controversial (even among those who associate with the Christian faith) ideas. Many other pastors and scholars have done these topics far better justice than I ever could anyway. But, regardless of your particular beliefs, my sincere prayer is that you keep an open mind about the things that are said in this book and see the beauty of Dad's life that was so well-lived.

I have made every effort to faithfully convey each portrait as best as I can without embellishing any details. Dad was a stickler for truth, and he passed that on to all of his children—I know he wouldn't want these stories told any other way. May the stories contained in the following pages manage to touch your life in the same positive way Dad's life touched others while he was here. I can think of no better way to honor his memory and the man he was than this.

God bless,
Tom Petz
May 25, 2015

"TO HEAR HIM TALK IN THAT MOMENT, IT WAS LIKE THE PAST 24 HOURS HAD NEVER HAPPENED."

Portrait 1

THE DAY AFTER EVERYTHING CHANGED

D AD fell asleep mid-sentence for what seemed like the hundredth time in the past hour. In a few minutes I knew he would wake again, ask me if he had nodded off, apologize, and attempt to continue his thought before falling asleep again a few minutes later.

Were the situation different, I may have gently chided Dad as I often would for not getting enough sleep or pushing himself too hard, which were activities he engaged in far too often. Dad never let his own tiredness get in the way of helping a friend or a member of his family. No matter how little time and energy he actually had, he *always* would find a way to help someone he cared about. As a result, however, it was not uncommon for Dad to be so fatigued that he would fall asleep at the dinner table or engage in a "power nap" while reading. Both amusing and endearing, we all became very used to the sight of Dad "just resting for a minute" in unexpected places and circumstances.

In the silence of the moment I recollected the seem-ingly endless number of times Dad had nodded off and pretended that this was just another one of those times he'd "overdone it" even though I knew in my heart it wasn't. A new reality was setting in for me on that grey and rainy day on Wednesday, October 15, 2014; Dad was not going to be with us for much longer.

It is one thing to process this intellectually and quite another to experience the hours, days, and weeks of it hap-pening. We had all known since Dad's diagnosis of aggres-sive stage 4 prostate cancer in the first half of 2010 that it was highly unlikely that he would die of "old age." But, up until early September of 2014, you would not have known there was anything wrong with him by the way he felt and acted. In fact, up until this point, he had never been hospi-talized because of the cancer!

Now, however, with him in a hospital bed, on heavy pain medications (which were the cause of his nodding off), and with a purple "Do Not Resuscitate" bracelet on his arm, there could be no question that the day we'd all dreaded for the past four-plus years was uncomfortably close.

My mom had called me in the afternoon the day before (Tuesday) to let me know that they were getting back from the doctor's office, and that they were going to be starting hospice care for Dad very soon. While the news saddened me, it did not surprise me—I had seen Dad at church on Sunday, and it was obvious he was growing increasingly uncomfortable and fatigued. I later found out that an Au-gust 12th visit to the doctor had shown that the cancer (which for years had been localized) had spread to nearly his entire body. Now, two months after that visit, the cancer was clearly taking its toll.

Just a few hours after the hospice phone call, Mom called me to let me know that Dad's condition had escalated rapidly, and that he was in so much pain that she was taking him to the emergency room. After hanging up the phone, we prayed for Dad as a family, shed a few tears, and I prepared to make my way to the hospital to meet up with Mom and other family members to lend what support I could.

As I was talking to my wife before heading out the door, our daughter came up to us with a look of utter peace and calm on her face. "Dad," she said "Papoh [our kids' nickname for my dad] will be all right. I just know it." I didn't know what to make of her words at that point, but I sensed that for that night, she had spoken a truth that we all very much needed to hear at that point.

The 30 mile drive from the apartment we were living in to the hospital was quiet, giving me time I needed to process what was happening and run through the numerous questions in my mind. What would I see when I arrived at the hospital? What would I say to my mom, to my dad, and to my siblings as we sat in the lobby at the ER waiting to find out exactly what was going on? Was this going to be just an overnight thing? Or, was this the beginning of a long and drawn out period of time where he was literally just waiting to die?

I met Mom in the waiting room where she filled me in on what was going on. The priority for the moment was to get Dad stabilized and out of pain. We'd be able to go back and see him—two people at a time—once the medications had had a chance to settle things down.

While we waited, my younger sister (who is a nurse) and her husband arrived at the hospital. In time, we got the word that Dad was stable enough to take visitors. My younger sister and my mom went first so she could provide my mom with her opinion on Dad's condition. Eventually, my sister came back and it was my turn to see Dad. So, I headed back through the confusing maze of the emergency room, eventually finding out where Dad was after a few minutes of searching.

Dad was in rough shape—clearly, the events of the day had been incredibly hard on him; he looked utterly exhausted. Mom was helping him suck on ice chips to help with the dehydration he was dealing with on top of the pain. While not fully coherent due to the pain medications, he said that he was getting a lot of relief. As he drained one IV bag and the nurse started him on another, some of his strength started to come back. Dad thanked me for making the trip out and being there for Mom. The three of us talked in the room for a while, while Mom did what she does best—doing everything she could to help Dad feel more comfortable.

I soon went back to the waiting room to send my younger brother (who had also arrived) back to see Dad. While he was back there, my mom came back and told me to go back and see him again. So, it was a meeting of Dad and his two sons. We encouraged Dad as best as we could, promised to be there for Mom, and he talked about how proud he was of the men we had become (and not for the first time that week). After telling him we loved him and would see him again soon, we headed back to the waiting room.

Several hours had now gone by at this point, and Mom started sending us kids home to rest and be with our families. As a group, we all felt that the worst was over for the night, and that Dad was going to be OK for now. I told Mom that I would head to the hospital the next day to visit and give her a break. Then, I headed home.

It was the events of the night before I reflected on as I waited for Dad to wake back up—the things we said, the things we saw, the new reality we were now facing head on. Literally just days earlier, Dad was getting around fairly well and talking about entering a new cancer wellness program. None of this seemed real—it had all happened way too fast.

Looking around the room, I noticed that there were a number of different candies and chocolates on the counter, which seemed odd. While Dad was in the candy business, the presence of a big pile of sweets in the room that he really couldn't eat puzzled me. When Dad woke up a few minutes later I asked him about it. "Those are to bless the nurses," he said, "to thank them for taking care of me." The thought of this made me laugh—here's a guy in serious condition with cancer and on heavy pain medications and he still had the presence of mind to make sure he did something nice for the nurses!

While Dad was sleeping, his phone had gone off several times because of emails he received. Ever diligent about taking care of his customers, he went through them methodically, deciding which to reply to and which he could reply to at a later time to save his energy. I mentioned to him that it may be better to just rest for a while and save his strength. The response was typical—agreement that this would probably indeed be a good idea, but wanting to get to "just one last email."

A visitor then showed up at the hospital to see Dad, and I went out to advise that this wasn't really the best time for him to have visitors. My mom, knowing how weak Dad was at this point, just wanted immediate family to have access to him so he could save his strength. Plus, he was in a hospital gown and bright yellow socks to keep his feet warm—not exactly "clothes for having company in."

As I was in the midst of explaining all of this and how tired Dad was to a very well-meaning and understanding visitor, Dad's cell phone rang. Before I could run back in there and tell him to let it go to voicemail, he answered it. What happened next stunned me.

To hear him talk in that moment, it was like the past 24 hours had never happened. Dad's voice had been slow and quiet all day, but now it was back with a vengeance, strong and confident. His mind was sharp again, and he laughed out loud several times in the conversation. The visitor I'd just got done telling that "Dad was too weak to see visitors" gave me a look like I was crazy—he was clearly fine! Listen to him in there—he didn't sound weak at all! I couldn't believe it—for the second time in less than an hour, I found myself thinking that none of this seemed real.

I walked the visitor down the hall, thanked them for their concern, promised to keep in touch, and went back into the room to see if something truly miraculous had happened to Dad while I was away. What I found was Dad sitting on the edge of the bed, breathing heavily through his breathing tubes and clearly completely wiped out. I helped him get back up onto the hospital bed and he asked who had come to visit. I told him, and he looked at me and asked a question I didn't expect: why I hadn't let the visitor come into the room? Incredulous, I asked him if he'd looked in the mirror in the past 15 seconds.

I then advised him of the irony of acting like he was as healthy as could be while I was actively advising people that he needed to rest and save his strength. He just looked at me and smiled, nodding slightly that he understood that maybe answering the phone hadn't been his best idea. As he drifted off to sleep again, I asked him why he had picked up the phone at all, or hadn't at the very least cut the conversation short. He smiled feebly and answered, "I didn't want them to be worried about me." And then he was gone again.

"No," I thought, "that is not what you would want at all."

Portrait 2

PERHAPS one of the more unusual things about Dad was that he only really worked for three companies in his life.

His first job was one he secured in his late teens— working for a home builder in the area where he lived. After he graduated high school, Dad briefly considered a career as a chemical engineer, but instead joined the family business, working there for over thirty years.

The family business was making candy—Dad's grandparents on his mother's side had started the business in the early 1900's, and his father and uncles had gradually grown it over the years. In that time, the company became known for never compromising on two things: the quality of their products and the care they took of their customers. While they didn't do everything perfectly, they did value things Dad valued, and I know he was proud of the different confections they made and sold.

Though Dad worked for a family business, he never acted as if he felt a sense of entitlement. He worked as hard or harder than anyone at the company. I have very early memories of Dad being gone before I got up, and arriving home well after the rest of us had been home from school for several hours. Many weekends, particularly during the company's busy season, Dad would work on Saturdays, arriving home in the early afternoon to do things with Mom or us kids. If I had to put a number on it, he probably worked at least 60-70 hours a week.

Dad didn't take a lot of vacation time either—maybe a week or two per year at most, even though as he earned higher and higher positions within the company, he could easily have justified more days off. That wasn't Dad, though —he wasn't one to ever complain or spend a lot of time thinking about how he could "get more." He felt fortunate to be able to do something he loved, with people he grew up with, that supported his family. The man rarely didn't have a smile in his face, even in the toughest of circumstances.

In time, several of the family members who were running the business began to retire, and transitioning the business to the next generation began in earnest. As a result of Dad's hard work and experience, he eventually became part owner in the company. As we kids we grew into our teens, we ended up joining him in his work, taking on part-time maintenance jobs and working in the retail store.

In many ways, working with Dad was great—we all got to see him more, for one thing. I would often stop in his office to see how he was doing, and he would always have lunch with us when we were at the office for a full day. Dad also made sure we were introduced around at the company, which eliminated some of the awkwardness that comes with starting a new job. I got to see first-hand the respect people had for Dad and the positive and edifying way he handled people and problems, which to this day is something I admire about him and continue to strive towards.

One thing that was evident to me very quickly, though, was that Dad drew pretty sharp distinctions between his work life and his personal life. It wasn't that he was a very different person while at work, it was that his priorities at work couldn't be the same priorities he had away from the office. At home, he was Dad, the family provider, defender, and the guy we could do fun stuff with. At work, he was responsible for helping to shape the direction of the company and for maintaining a productive workforce. I struggled at times with his "dual identity," and even had a lot of confusion about whether I should call him "Dad" while we were at work (often avoiding the issue entirely by resorting to other ways to get his attention). Honestly, even as I was preparing to leave the company after having been there for several years, it was still an area that I struggled with.

After I'd been gone a while, I noticed that my brother and sisters (who were all still with the company) started referring to Dad as "JP," which is what Dad had started calling himself. Ironically, this was a few years after the music artist Prince had asked that he be referred to by a symbol, so I always thought this was all a bit weird. Here is a man in his forties all of a sudden giving himself a nickname seemingly out of nowhere—I often wondered if he was he having a midlife crisis! But, it turns out that there is a story behind the change that is so "Dad."

The company had recently hired a new salesperson who had a name that sounded an awful lot like Dad's, especially when it was said in a phone call. So, people would call the office looking for the salesperson, and the well-meaning operator would sometimes mis-hear and accidentally direct the phone call to Dad and vice-versa. Dad eventually grew tired of this, and decided that instead of getting mad at the operator or telling the salesperson to make a change, that the easiest and most logical way to deal with the problem was for him to take on the name of "JP" so that the names wouldn't be confused anymore. And thus, "JP" was born, and this became the name everyone called him by— even us kids.

I'd be lying, though, if I said that I didn't personally feel like something more familiar and personal was lost by referring to Dad as "JP" all the time. As awkward as it was to use the name "Dad" at work, it was equally awkward for me to use the name "JP" while he was at home. So, for me, the solution for both situations was to always address him in a specific way based on where I was with him. Any time we were together in a work or professional context, I referred to him as "JP." Any other time, he was simply "Dad."

In my mind, then, "JP" became the persona Dad took on whenever he was at work. That was the man whose priority was business strategy, budgets, long hours, and the respect of the people he worked with. Whenever I used the name "JP," it was a mental reminder to me that I was talking to someone who didn't necessarily have his "Dad" hat on at the time. This helped me a lot through the years, especially when I had the occasional consulting arrangement with his work.

As years passed, the company began to experience some problems that required some difficult decisions to be made. Market conditions and management dynamics conspired together to force some major changes at the company. Some big mistakes occurred. Consultants were brought in. New ideas and investment capital were sought. Family members, including my brothers and sisters, finished school and left the company. As part owner in the company, "JP" knew he had a responsibility to fix things as best as he could. And he did so, methodically working through the myriad of problems with all of the new faces to make decisions that would ensure the company's long-term viability. However, he soon found himself being in the unenviable position of being the last family member standing with both an ownership stake in the company and day-to-day responsibilities with respect to leading it.

Things began to come to a head in late winter of 2009 when I received a phone call from Dad—he told me he needed some advice about his work situation. He explained to me what was going on and his growing feeling that his presence was a source of tension for the company's new CEO—that he felt he was getting in his way. We talked about whether he should stay with the company he'd been with for thirty years and had poured almost his whole life into or if it was time for him to step aside as everyone else in the family had. And, if indeed now was the time to move on, how would he deal with the "ownership" issue? Would a departure be seen as a vote of no confidence in the new CEO, a person Dad felt, despite their differences, was a good man and deserved a chance? How could he be sure that if he left, it was for the right reasons?

As we talked, it became more and more evident that very soon, he would need to leave the company in order for it to move forward with its new leadership team. It was just time. While many of the logistics of his impending departure were still up in the air, the conversation then turned to what he would do next. Dad had an idea for a new company that he thought could work. He would run it himself out of his home and the company's business model would be able to leverage his extensive experience and broad contacts in the candy making industry. However, success was far from certain—the economy was tanking, the business model he'd come up with was a bit off the beaten path, and it would be roughly a year before the business made any significant money. Plus, Dad had a mortgage to pay and was about ten years from retirement. Suffice it to say, many of us questioned whether or not starting a business at that point in his life was really the best idea!

But, one thing about Dad is that once he got an idea in his head, it was hard to talk him out of it. In the months that followed our conversation, he worked out an exit strategy from the family business and began laying the groundwork for the new company he had envisioned, a company that would have his stamp all over it ... including the nickname "JP" in its name.

While others may disagree agree with me, I feel that this is where the nickname Dad had given himself years ago to solve a problem really became something more than just a name. "JP" became an identity for both him and his company—what his values were, a commitment to customers, exciting ideas, and excellence in everything he did.

For the next year, "JP" worked tirelessly to build the company he'd envisioned, and this became the third company he worked for in his life. He traveled a lot. He was always on the phone. He was constantly refining ideas and meeting new people. And, the company was showing signs that it was going to work out. In just about a year, "JP" was well on his way to turning his vision into a viable reality.

But then, in May of 2010, after a routine physical, he received news none of us saw coming. It was bad—cancer. Stage 4. Aggressive. Inoperable. Incurable. Fatal.

I didn't know it at the time, but Dad's original prognosis was that he had about six months to live (an estimate he ended up beating by a wide margin). Just about a year into forming his company and as it was starting to work, "JP" was at a major crossroads. The uncertainty he'd started this venture with was all of a sudden magnified a hundredfold. Is this what he wanted to spend his remaining time on earth doing?

How "JP" came to the conclusion that he should continue on with his plan to start a company, I'll never know, but that is exactly what he did. This was a decision he never regretted, by the way—he often said that as much as he loved working for the family business, his five-plus years being on his own were the best of his life. He truly loved the work and the people he worked with.

As the new company grew, "JP" customers began to know his story and had to know that, regardless of how healthy he appeared at the time, that sooner rather than later, the cancer was going to take "JP's" life from him. But somehow the uncertainty that you would think would be associated with "knowing the facts" didn't seem to matter all that much; people didn't see a cancer patient when they looked at Dad. They saw "JP," a man who was all of those things I mentioned plus one more thing—a person who had every reason to give up, but didn't. They saw a vision of someone worth investing in, and they did.

In that way, "JP" came to be not just Dad's identity or his company's identity, but the identity of the ever-growing community of people he associated with. In the end, "JP" did pass away, but the company he started and the people whose lives he touched and inspired through his example live on and continue to thrive. "JP" lives on!

Portrait 3

WIND MAN

I T is getting close to dinner time on a beautiful August afternoon, nearly ten months to the day after Dad lost his battle with cancer. Outside, the temperature is in the upper seventies, the sun is shining, and the wind is blowing through the pine trees, making their branches lazily sway back and forth in an evergreen version of "the wave." I am outside on the front porch taking it all in while working on finishing another section of this story, not having to think too hard about what Dad would normally have been doing on a day like this one. There is no doubt that he would have been out on his sailboat, engaging in one of his favorite pastimes. I allow myself a moment to imagine he is out on the lake right now, puttering around and trying to figure out how to get a little extra speed out of his boat — a thought that brings a smile to my face as I continue to write.

The sudden sound of a new text message arriving interrupts my current train of thought, a train I realize was already in the process of getting derailed anyway due to the craziness of the day. I decide take a break to pick up my phone and read: "Tom, I was thinking of the wind blowing so beautiful today. And then I thought of your dad and what a privilege it is to know him. I sense him from Heaven cheering on me, you and so many others!!"

The message is from a pastor of a very large church in the area, who was a close friend of Dad's. I actually hadn't talked to him since Dad's funeral, where he offered some extremely touching testimony about their friendship and what Dad meant to him. He also helped us in a big way with getting the memorial service itself arranged. He is a very good man, and his acts of kindness towards our family during a very difficult time are things we will all be forever grateful for. And now, completely out of the blue, this man with thousands of parishioners and undoubtedly countless "church worries" on his mind sends me a message about how he's thinking about Dad today.

The gesture is overwhelming generous to me, and I start to tear up a little at the awesome "coincidence" of this message coming to me at exactly the perfect time. What this man cannot know is that I am working through some health issues and significant adversity at work right now. God does, though, and since He is constantly at work for His people (Romans 8:28, one of Dad's favorite Bible passages), I recognize that He is using this pastor's message to remind me that that I've got two loving Fathers in Heaven in my corner telling me to keep going. This is encouragement my spirit needs today, a day when there's a weight on me that feels far too heavy.

Through my still slightly blurry eyes, I read over the text message again "I was thinking of the wind blowing so beautiful today. And then I thought of your dad..." I realize then that there's something else that God is giving me through this pastor without him knowing it, thoughts and ideas that are perfect for what I should write in this portrait of Dad.

I send him back, "You know, it's funny. I am sitting on the porch right now in the wind, writing some thoughts down about Dad and his life. He would have loved a day like this... Dad is still with all of us. Days like this are a great reminder of that!"

I chuckle as my thoughts again turn back to Dad. He is the only guy I know who would be flattered to know that a day with a steady wind blowing was all it took to get people thinking about him. There are just too many wrong ways something like this could go (ask any twelve year old boy). But for Dad, it is the type of association he would totally embrace. You needed the wind in order to sail, and sailing was a huge part of Dad's life and identity—literally everyone he associated with knew how much he loved the sport. He had images of sailboats everywhere—in his home, his office, and even on his company's logo. He was a man known for judging the quality of a summer day on two things: what the wind was doing and how bright the sunshine was, in that order. On days with particularly favorable conditions, you could take for granted that Dad was so excited you would have thought he'd just won the lottery; it was a great day to go sailing.

That Dad developed such a passion for sailing at all is somewhat surprising. He didn't grow up in a family of sailors, or even boaters for that matter. There was his grandparents' cottage he would visit from time to time that was on the water, but his childhood was mostly as a "land-lubber"—on tractors, working in the yard with his dad, and spending time on building projects. However, there was something about sailing and being out on the water that drew Dad in like a magnet, whispering "come" into his soul like a warm summer breeze. It was a call he couldn't ignore, and sailing quickly became his go-to activity for when he wanted to relax.

Like many "enthusiasts," Dad fueled his zeal for the wind and waves by owning many sailboats in his life—each was different, in much the same way people are different. Some boats were big, some were small. Some were geared to go as fast as possible, others more geared for a slower, more easy-going, pace. Some were designed for one or two people, some could accommodate many more. Dad, in the same way he enjoyed all different types of people, enjoyed each boat for its distinct qualities—valuing each one for their different adventures, challenges, and memories.

For instance, there was the Mallard, a boat that will always stand out for a number of reasons. It was the first sailboat Dad owned on his own, for one thing, and has a story behind its purchase that is rather ... unique. This boat Dad trailered around, often sailing around on inland lakes until he gained enough confidence to sail on bigger lakes. Eventually, Mom and Dad came to own a house on Lake Huron, and the boat ended up being stored on a trailer on the beach in front of the house. As the boat was pretty heavy, Dad engineered an incredibly clever winch system for getting the boat in and out of the water. The boat could be sailed with one or two people pretty easily, though it could certainly hold several more comfortably. Dad learned a lot on that boat, and it wasn't long before we kids were joining him for afternoons out on the lake. My brother and I, in particular, grew as attached to sailing and that boat as Dad was.

That's why it was pretty devastating for all of us when it eventually sunk. Dad had launched the boat from the beach earlier in the day, but as often happens on the water, the weather changed quickly. A cold front whipped through the area, bringing with it a very strong north wind that had churned the waves on the lake into a mad frenzy. Putting the boat back on the trailer that day was impossible—it was much too dangerous to try and attempt something like that, especially with small children running around. So, Dad anchored the boat just offshore in shallow water as best as he could and figured he would get it back onto the trailer when the wind calmed down. Unfortunately, he never got the chance—the weather intensified and the wind and waves conspired together to rip the cover whose job it was to keep water from entering the sailboat. Once that happened, things escalated quickly and the boat sank, spending hours grinding on the bottom of the lake, resulting in the appearance of a large hole in the bottom of the boat. It was ruined.

Dad wasn't defeated, however, and that boat sinking became an opportunity to explore grander sailing visions (much to the chagrin of Mom, who had long since decided that sailing was not for her). His next boat was significantly larger than his first one was but still trailer-able, and it had sleeping quarters, which we kids were extremely excited about. And even though this boat was far from fast, it was during the years that we had this boat that Dad first started to share his dream for doing sailboat racing someday.

After a few years with that boat, Dad sold it and took a break from larger, trailered sailboats. Instead, we sailed from much smaller boats we simply dragged up and down the beach. It was on these beach boats that my brother and I really learned how to sail—Dad was a good teacher, and we quickly learned not only all of the sailing-related jargon, but important rules on the water and how to ride the wind from point A to point B.

As our skills grew with smaller boats, Dad began to talk more and more about his dream to do sailboat racing. My brother and I were "all in" at this point, as was our uncle and a few of our friends. We found an unbelievable deal on a boat that was suitable for racing and we joined a yacht club that had a well-developed sailing program. We were on our way!

It turns out, though, that while those years on smaller boats were helpful in developing core sailing skills, we were pretty awful at competitive sailing and as a result, we performed incredibly poorly for quite a while. Dad tried to stay positive, but as a pretty competitive guy, it was clear that he absolutely *hated* losing all the time. He spent hours studying sailing books and magazines, learning about everything he could about sail shape and the importance of acronyms that we'd never heard before of like VMG (Velocity Made Good) and COG (Course Over Ground).

In time and in no small part due to Dad's competitive spirit, we got a lot better and we started winning the occasional race. Encouraged and gaining confidence by the day through our progress, we soon coined a new acronym—Grins Per Dollar (GPD), a function of the (relatively small) amount of money we'd spent on the boat and the number of smiles it brought to our faces. As we began to win more and more races, GPD became extremely high for all of us, particularly for Dad, who was extremely proud of how far the sailing team had come. But just being successful wasn't enough for Dad. Now that we were into competitive sailing and doing well at it, he began to dream about doing long distance races, in particular the Port Huron-to-Mackinac race. The only problem? The boat we currently sailed was too small to compete. Talk of getting a bigger boat became a regular topic of conversation, and soon became a reality when the mast on the boat we had started racing with snapped in half, totaling it.

After a couple of months of searching, we found the perfect sailboat for us to continue racing with. It was cheap, was big enough to do long distance races on, and had been competitive in sailboat racing in the past. We couldn't wait to get it into the water and start winning races with it.

As the new racing season began, however, we quickly discovered that the sailing knowledge we'd gained on the smaller racing boat would not help us much on this one that was new to us. We were awful again. Undaunted by this setback, Dad got to work, exploring every nook and cranny he could to coax more speed out of the boat. It seemed to come slower this time, though, and we were very hit and miss with how we finished. Sometimes we were in the hunt with the top boats in the fleet, other times we were dead last by a mile.

When we found ourselves hopelessly behind the rest of the boats in the fleet, that became our opportunity to try different things on the boat to make it go faster. I think that for Dad, doing this kind of experimentation was just as good as racing for first place—he was a constant fidgeter and relished moving around the boat, pulling every last line he could to see what might happen.

In one race I will never forget, we ended up ridiculously far behind by the time we were completing the first leg of the race. It was very windy, the lake incredibly choppy, and we didn't have enough guys on the boat to keep it flat (which was crucial if we wanted to do well). We watched in agony as boat after boat completed the first leg of the race ahead of us. We felt at that point that we'd set a new record for the shortest amount of time it had taken for us to enter experimentation mode.

The next leg of the race was what sailors call a "downwind" run. That is, both the wind and the boat are on the same straight line, heading in the same direction. Usually when sailing downwind, sailors will hoist brightly colored, balloon-like sails up called "spinnakers" in order to catch as much air as possible and make the boat go faster.

However, sometime before we needed to start the downwind part of the race, one of us noticed that none of the other boats were putting their spinnakers up due to the high winds and rough seas. Figuring we had nothing to lose and everything to gain, we decided to put our spinnaker up and see if we could catch the rest of the boats in front of us. What happened next surprised all of us. Once the spinnaker went up, there was a loud BOOM and the boat took off like a missile. It was fast, hair raising, and more than little bit out of control, but Dad loved it, and the smile and laughter on his face as we flew past boat after boat was contagious. None of us had ever done something like that or gone that fast on a sailboat before. It was a pretty exhilarating experience! Suffice it to say, the experiment of hoisting a spinnaker when no one else dared to ended up paying off, and we got back into the race, ultimately winning it by a huge margin. To this day, it is one of my favorite memories sailing with Dad.

But, as fun as that experience and the many races after it were, they couldn't last forever.

Dad used to have a piece of sailing-themed inspirational paraphernalia in his office that said something like this: "We cannot change the direction of the wind, but we can adjust our sails." In other words, life often hits us from unexpected and often completely unhelpful directions; get used to it. Dad seemed to understand this very well, possibly as a result of his experiences on the water and his accidentally destroyed watercraft. He never bemoaned this truth; he just accepted it as part of life and dealt with it accordingly, often discovering new oceans in the process.

And so, soon after Dad realized his dream of doing a Port Huron-to-Mackinac race on the boat, his "big boat" racing career began the process of slowly winding down. Dad had to face some practical realities like the fact that I had gotten married and had a family to take care of as well as the time and expense it took to keep racing and be competitive at it. When he was eventually diagnosed with cancer, Dad officially "retired," knowing it was time to refocus his energies and set sail for something else.

That doesn't mean he quit sailing, though. Instead he decided to get into competitive small-boat racing, and it turned out to be Dad's last great sailing adventure. He, my brother, and a few like-minded friends decided to start a sail club headquartered at the house my parents owned on the lake. Everyone in the club just sailed from the beach out to a race course my brother or another member of the club would set up. The boats they sailed were cheap, enabling all different sorts of people to participate and assuring high Grins Per Dollar for everyone. The races were fun, fast, and friendly, and the new sailing arrangement allowed Dad to spend more time with family and friends while conserving his energy. Dad leveraged his enormous amount of sailing experience and was one of the top sailors in the fleet, an accomplishment he was very proud of. He and my brother even made a couple of trips south to be in various regional sailing competitions, where again, he proved his sailing mettle against tough competition.

I doubt that when Dad originally started sailing that he gave any thought to it becoming such a perfect metaphor for his life. He lived his life as he sailed his boats—at all times with a giant grin on his face regardless of what boat he was on or other circumstances. The man always had an awareness of what the wind was doing and he was always chasing it and then adjusting to it in both a literal and figurative sense.

I often think that it would have been a lot easier not to be like that, to play it safe and only sail in "favorable conditions." It is hard to understand why someone would live with such wild, almost reckless, abandon for things with so little certainty attached to them. Yet Dad lived and thrived living that way both on the water and in his relationships with other people. He was infinitely flexible; it didn't matter what happened. He went after it and he helped people. He chased them down so they knew he cared about them. It wasn't for the faint of heart, and sometimes he got burned, but time and again he found the strength to adjust his sails and keep moving forward. I have often wondered how he was able to live this way so consistently.

In the midst of pondering this, I receive another message from the pastor who had texted me earlier that gives me a clue: "Tom, I read Psalm 104. It's about God riding on the winds! Awesome, you have to read it." I grab my Bible and start to read, stumbling across this passage:

> *He makes the clouds his chariot*
> > *and rides on the wings of the wind.*
> *He makes wind his messengers*
> > *flames of fire his servants.*

Then it hits me. Dad chased the wind because he knew that's where God is; it is how he got closer to his Creator, where he felt most alive. He practiced chasing the wind on the water so he could reflect this behavior in every other aspect of his life. And, could it be that the more he "chased the wind," the bigger God got to him? Is it any wonder that the joy expressed at the end of the Psalm 104 and the joy I know was always in Dad's heart seem so similar? Is the picture the pastor had in his mind of Dad encouraging us from Heaven a call for all of us to chase the wind like he did so we find the same God he found, the same joy? Doesn't it just make sense that now that he's with God, Dad would have a pretty unique perspective on this?

As I reflect on these questions, I receive one last text message: "Your dad understood that Psalm. He lived it. To people your dad was like the wind bringing God's care to every person he encountered. He was a Wind Man!"

Yes, in every sense of the word, he was.

Portrait 4

BUILDER

I remember an article I read some years ago in the *Reader's Digest* called "Dad Will Build It."[1] The article was written from the perspective of a daughter fondly recalling her father's gift for creating beautiful things with his bare hands and the impact that gift had on her relationship with him. When I read it, I knew exactly what she was talking about—Dad was the same way.

Dad grew up with a father who was constantly doing things to the house; the man never seemed to run out of energy or big ideas. As the eldest son in a family of ten kids, Dad was often called upon to be an extra pair of hands when it came time to start another home improvement project. I suspect Dad loved this as much as his dad did—there is something about fathers and sons working together with their hands that creates powerful, almost sacred, bonds and memories that last for a lifetime. There's a sense

---

1 http://www.rd.com/true-stories/inspiring/greatest-gift-dad-daughter/

of pride looking at a finished project and knowing that it was done right and completed with your own blood, sweat, and tears.

It was in the years working on those projects that Dad learned the value of being able to tackle a job yourself and a love of working with his hands to create wondrous things out of raw materials. He also developed an appreciation for what it meant to do a job not just "to code," but perfectly. His dad was a stickler for details and uncompromising when it came to quality, and he made sure to impart this philosophy onto Dad.

It is logical, then, that Dad's first "real" job was working for a local builder, where he was able to take the skills he had grown up with and use them to make some money. It was in this job where Dad's knowledge of building was taken to a whole other level; during his time working on a construction crew, he learned just about everything he could about the building trade. At first, he was the kid whose job it was to haul wood around or lift heavy shingles up a ladder and get them onto a roof that was going in. The work was exhausting, but it built muscles onto Dad's wiry frame, muscles he was soon to need as he graduated on to more advanced construction tasks like nailing walls together and lifting them into place for hours and hours at a time.

Dad also learned about building codes and how to wire plugs, lights, and switches. He developed an eye for a well-built foundation—the value of solid footings and straight walls. He learned about putting up drywall, and how to mud and tape seams. He learned about insulation and plumbing, HVAC and trim work. He learned it all and got extremely skilled at doing each job in a very short amount of time.

As good as Dad was at construction work, he knew it was not going to be the career he spent the rest of his life on, and it wasn't long before he joined the family candy business. However, Dad didn't let the things he'd picked up go to waste; on the contrary, Dad spent the rest of his life tackling some massive building and remodeling projects. His first was a doozy—building a house for himself and Mom.

Now when I say "house," what I should say is "garage," because in truth, that's what Dad built, at least at first. Mom and Dad had gotten married at nineteen, and as one might expect, this meant that they didn't have a whole lot of money to spend on a home. What they did have was a plot of land Dad's father had given them as a wedding present and a plan that would end most marriages before they were given a fair a chance to start—Dad would build a garage on the land they had been given, and the garage would be the temporary house Mom and Dad lived in while Dad built their "real" house. Oh, and Dad would do the bulk of this work himself, with some help from a well driller, an excavator, a cement guy, and some family members along the way.

If this plan sounds like utter madness to you, you are not alone. The reality of it is that Dad started this project while he was still in his teens, after only spending a relatively short amount of time in the construction business. I think most rational people would be scared or intimidated by a project of that scope and size, but not Dad. He and Mom got to work digging the footings for the "garage" themselves by hand in a spot that "seemed like a good place" and they were on their way.

In time, the garage was completed, and phase two of the project was soon put into motion. Money was understandably still tight, so Mom and Dad made "walls" in the garage with spare cardboard boxes Dad had grabbed from work. Soon, my older sister was born and she joined them in their humble but "cozy" temporary dwelling. Months continued to tick by while slow but steady progress on their "real" home continued.

The house Dad was building was from one of those home building kits that were extremely popular in the early twentieth century. The kits supplied plans and a lot of pre-cut lumber; the rest was left up to the purchaser. A characteristic of these plans was that most of the framing could be done with one person—ideal for Dad since often, Mom (who had no skilled trades experience and had a baby girl to take care of) was often his sole source of assistance. Eventually, though, the work was done and Mom and Dad were finally able to move into their brand new home.

Dad must have felt an intense sense of pride and relief when the house was complete. The house was built his way, and had a couple of his special touches in it, such as a basement fireplace, an airtight wood storage box that allowed someone to add logs to the fire from inside the house without making a mess, and a really nice deck off of the main floor. The house was also built into a hill, so the basement had a walk out area and lots of windows that brought in plenty of natural light. We kids spent hours and hours playing out in the large yard, riding on tractors, biking trails, sledding on hills, and skating on the nearby pond. It was the perfect place to raise a young family.

The house was not without its quirks, however. Dad had reversed the hot and cold supply lines to the upstairs bathroom by mistake, which caused hot water to come out the opposite of what you might expect. Also, there was a staircase to the upstairs Mom was not particularly fond of —Dad had left the risers off of the steps, which gave the staircase an open feel, but each step had enough space between it for a small child to slip between and fall to their doom.

But, it was home, and because Mom and Dad had been frugal with building it, they were not saddled with massive amounts of debt. This, in turn, allowed them to purchase my great-grandmother's home on Lake Huron when she was no longer able to take care of it.

I remember during the days in that first home thinking that all of this would last forever, but inevitably, it didn't. Dad had a very long commute to work every day (roughly an hour), and Mom and Dad increasingly wanted to spend time at the house on the lake, which was about two hours away. The large yard required a lot of hours on a tractor in order to keep up. So, they made the difficult decision to move from the home they'd built themselves into something that would be both closer to Dad's work and to the lake house.

I think it's interesting that after the experience Dad had getting started, he never built another house again. In truth, it never even seemed to cross his mind, perhaps because of how hard it was the first time, the stress of his job, or the demands of a young family. Perhaps it was a combination of all three of these things. Regardless, once the decision was made to move, we began the long process of looking for a new home to live in.

This didn't prove to be easy—we kids really did not want to move at all, and we were not willing to settle for houses with small yards or no pool to swim in. Moreover, the house had to have the right "look" to it, both inside and out. Mom and Dad had their own set of non-negotiable conditions—location, price, condition of the house, etc.

We eventually found a place that made us all happy, and we moved in just before Christmas in 1985. It wasn't long after that we discovered that the house had a few problems that needed to be addressed. And by a few, I mean that for the longest time, we thought that the movie *The Money Pit* was about our adventures with the new home. Any thoughts Mom and Dad had that purchasing something pre-built was going to be an easier road were quickly annihilated—it turned out that buying a home was just about as much work as building one.

The first thing we discovered as the winter snows melted and the spring rains began was that the river that formed the rear boundary of the property had a tendency to overflow into the back yard every so often. This, in turn, made the sump pump in the house run constantly. And because it was running all of the time, it eventually burned itself out, resulting in a partially flooded basement.

The winter we'd moved in had also not been kind to the pool; it was completely destroyed and had to be removed and replaced. The heating and cooling system for the house turned out to be inadequate and on its last legs, so new systems were installed. The stairway down to the pool was full of rotten wood and had to be rebuilt. After a few years, the relatively flat roof on the house had begun to leak and needed to be redesigned and rebuilt. The rather long black-top driveway in front of the house only lasted a season or two before big machines had to come in, tear it out, and put down new asphalt. The septic tank drain field had to be dug up, where we discovered that a giant rock had busted one of the pipes.

Dealing with those problems and more certainly kept Dad busy, but he took on a number of home improvement projects for the house too. Dad built shelves and put paneling in the basement, providing storage and added living space. New landscaping went in, and Dad completely re-did the lawn in the back yard. Dad also figured out a way to make a skating pond by leveling a section of the back yard, laying some greenhouse plastic down, and pumping cold water from the river into the area. He even ran lights to the makeshift pond and devised an incredibly clever system for draining it when the spring came. If all of that weren't enough, Dad managed to drop a new bathroom into the room that my brother and I shared so we would have an extra shower in the house and we wouldn't have to go so far down the hallway to use the bathroom.

As one might imagine, not everything went perfectly, like the time Dad was running the plumbing for the new bathroom my brother and I were to share. Unfortunately, he didn't solder the pipes right so when he turned the water on, he got a quite unexpected and cold shower in the middle of the basement! I still remember him standing there getting rained on with an expression of utter exasperation and disgust on his face. But, Dad got right to fixing it as he always did, never getting too down about a setback, and always driving forward through the hassles.

While Dad worked on all of these projects, he made sure to teach his sons all he knew about building things. He talked over ideas with us, he took us to the store, he taught us the names of tools and how to use them, and most importantly, he had us help him with the work. While we thought we were just doing something cool, Dad was preparing us to be men who could take care of own homes someday. We also learned that no problem was unfixable—Dad had a gift for sizing up a problem and figuring out the best way to handle it. No problem intimidated him—he could build anything and make any issue he encountered right.

Ironically, just about as we were finishing the last of the projects on the house we'd moved to, Mom and Dad decided to move again. The upkeep on the house we were living in was getting to be too much for everyone—all of us kids were entering our teenage years and we began to have other priorities and jobs of our own that left little time to help Mom and Dad out. So, we packed up a semi-truck and were off once more, this time to a newer house that wouldn't need as much work as the one we were living in had needed. Sure, there were a couple of big projects Dad tackled, like finishing the basement, fixing a major water leak in the basement, fixing the roof, and building a really cool hangout area in the basement out of a sailboat we'd wrecked, but by and large, the newer house was a lot less work.

As it turned out, that was a good thing for all of us kids. As we began to move out and into homes of our own, we found ourselves purchasing "fixer-uppers"—homes we could afford but still needed a lot of work. Dad helped every one of us quite a bit with our own home improvement projects, and was a constant source of encouragement to my brother and me as we began to tackle bigger projects of our own. Both our confidence and our home improvement repertoire grew with the completion of each successful project—roof teardowns and rebuilds, gutting rooms, bathroom renovations, you name it.

We all, though, eventually reached a point where all of our "do-it-yourself" home improvement projects began to wind down. This happened for a variety of reasons, but in my case it really came down to the fact that I really didn't have the time or energy for such initiatives anymore because of stress at work and wanting to spend more recreation time with my family. So, while we did have some major construction projects to get done like a kitchen remodel, we almost exclusively used contractors to get the work done.

It was around this time that all of our construction projects began to wane that Dad received his cancer diagnosis. I remember thinking at that point that it was a really good thing that the family home improvement projects were coming to a close, as I expected Dad's energy levels to be depleted because of the cancer treatments he was inevitably going to need to undergo. I think we all wanted him to save his strength for trying to get well and enjoying whatever time he had left on this earth as much as possible.

But, as usual, Dad had other plans. That house Mom and Dad had bought on the lake all those years ago? Dad gutted it down to the framing, re-doing everything from scratch. New plumbing, insulation, radiant floor heating (including a ridiculous heat exchanger he assembled himself somehow), wiring, windows, and drywall went in. New flooring and cabinetry was ordered and installed. It was the largest renovation Dad had tackled in some time, and he did so as a cancer patient.

Meanwhile, he was pushing Mom to make one last move to a smaller home that would be ideal for their "empty-nest" years. The only problem was that the real estate market in the area was a shambles at that point. But, they persevered and eventually an older home that met their needs became available. The home needed a lot of work, but that didn't intimidate Dad. He got right to work, tearing apart floors and bathrooms, and everything in between. For a while, the only working bathroom they had in the house was in the basement—not ideal when your bedroom is on the second floor of the house and you have to make several trips down there during the night to pee.

Thus, in his "cancer patient" years Dad had not just one, but two massive home remodeling projects to work on. At a time when most people would be trying to do less work in order to save their strength, Dad had doubled down.

As all of this was taking place, my wife and kids and I were also just getting started on a project of our own. For years, I had been pining after the home of my younger days with skating ponds and tractors and wooded spaces. But, because of where we lived and the state of the housing market, finding a home that would meet our needs affordably proved to be impossible. Frustrated, we began to embark on a course of action I once swore I would never attempt—we decided to purchase a piece of property while land values and interest rates were at rock bottom and build a custom home within a few years.

I knew I couldn't build the home myself like Dad had done, but thanks to him, I knew what to look for when we went looking for a builder when the time came to start construction. And we found one who was perfect—he spoke the language Dad did about straight walls, careful planning, and building things strong. Work soon commenced on the project, and we were on our way.

Even though Dad had two major home renovations going on, he still found time to visit me out at the build site on a regular basis. Being new to the home building process, I asked his opinion on everything, and he'd freely give it, saying things like "Wow, he pea graveled the entire basement—we never used to do that when we built houses" and "It looks like you're going to have nine-foot ceilings on the main floor; most builders won't just do that unless you ask." Dad shared his input on the overall design of the home. He took a tape measure to walls and made sure they were square. He complimented the very neat work the electricians and plumbers had done. He inspected all of the building materials to make sure they were straight and strong.

On Dad's last trip to the house before he died, he was in declining health but still managed to enthusiastically move around the still unfinished home, pointing out things he noticed that impressed him and asking questions about finishes and projects that were still a work in progress. As we were preparing to leave, Dad said something I wasn't aware I was waiting to hear until he said it. "You know, when you first told me your plans to build this place I worried for you because I know how hard it is and how many bad contractors there are out there. But, walking around this place—son, you found the right guy to build your house; he's done a great job and you're going to love living here."

In that moment, I realized that Dad's approval of the house meant everything to me, and now I had it. The house still had several weeks to go before it was complete, but it had something on it now that had been missing, yet was vitally important to have—his blessing, behind it an entire lifetime of building things to extremely high standards.

After Dad passed away, I carried his words with me every time I went to the house to see how things were going. Without Dad, there was now a certain level of anxiety and uncertainty in me that hadn't been there before. But, I knew it was all going to be OK. After all, Dad had said so, and man, could he ever build things.

"THERE'S NO QUESTION DAD WAS A VISIONARY—BUT ANY GOOD VISIONARY WILL TELL YOU THEY NEED TO BE BROUGHT BACK DOWN TO EARTH EVERY SO OFTEN..."

Portrait 5

"SORRY, CUTIE"

F ROM the moment Mom walked into the house, I knew Dad was in trouble. Originally, the plan was to remove a load bearing wall on the main floor of the lake house my parents had purchased from my mother's grandmother back in the 1980s and replace it with a manufactured beam. The grand vision was to open up the whole space and renovate it, which everyone agreed was a great idea. Removing the wall and adding the beam was supposed to be a quick and simple "end of summer" project to get the renovation started so that in subsequent years, we'd be freed up to tackle other parts of the overall plan.

However, as anyone who has done a home improvement project could tell you, things are rarely ever that simple. After the wall was removed, the crew working to install the new beam discovered that plumbing from the upstairs bathroom was exactly where the new beam needed to go. Dad wisely got Mom involved and they agreed that they would now need to tackle a fairly small bathroom teardown and rebuild in order to enable the beam project to get done successfully.

But that had been months ago—we were now standing in a wide open space in the middle of winter with all of the drywall down, the ceiling gone, wires everywhere, new insulation going up, and an entirely new radiant floor heating system going in throughout the entire house. And, it turns out, Dad hadn't exactly briefed Mom on all of these details or the greatly expanded costs of the extra work yet. Oops.

Mom didn't yell or get mad at Dad right then—that isn't how she does things—but the look on her face told me there was going to be a pretty direct conversation later that night about how on earth replacing a beam and fixing up a bathroom turned into a teardown and rebuild of the entire main floor of the house.

While I didn't know exactly what Dad was going to say in that conversation to explain himself, there was one thing I knew he would say because I'd heard him say it over and over when he had managed to put himself in similar awkward spots: "Sorry, Cutie."

―――――

I am not sure how old I was or what Dad had done the first time I'd heard him say "Sorry, Cutie," but it was phrase he used when he knew he had no defense for something he had done that in his mind was was "no big deal," but *in truth* he needed to spend more time thinking through with Mom's input.

Oh, there were almost always warning signs that we all (Mom, in particular) tried to get Dad to pay attention to, but he would politely dismiss such talk as "worrying too much" or "just being ridiculous." It wasn't at all that Dad was particularly prideful, thoughtless, or caught up with himself; it was that he would often get way too excited about the vision he was pursuing and forget about "little details" like budgets, other priorities, how long it would take to actually accomplish something, or things that could potentially go disastrously wrong.

There's no question Dad was a visionary—but any good visionary will tell you they need to be brought back down to earth every so often or they have a tendency to make some colossal errors in judgment. Mom was ideally positioned to be that person for Dad—but she didn't always get a chance to have her say until it was too late...

———————

Picture the process of building a brand new home from scratch. Not only do you need to get the home built up to code, but you've got to pick out all of the wall and window treatments, every doorknob, every light fixture, etc. It's a lot of late nights, fast food, and endless hours of discussing such things as whether you should go with "chardonnay" or "vintage wine" stone for the fireplace. It's exhausting and stressful and most significantly, costly.

Sometimes, you get to the point where you're ready to start living in the new home and you don't have as much money as you thought you would have due to issues that came up during construction or life things that can just

happen sometimes. Maybe you were on a shoestring bud-
get to begin with. Whatever the reason, inevitably, conversations take place, you decide what you can and cannot live
without, and you put onto the back burner those projects
that are not absolutely essential to living in the house. It
happens all the time.

That was the position my parents found themselves in
as they were moving into the home Dad had just finished
building for the family. It had all of the essentials and was
quite cozy, but one thing they knew was that putting in car-
peting on the main floor was going to have to wait until
some money was freed up. So, Mom and Dad just made due
with what they had; in a few short months, the problem
would be taken care of once they'd had some time to save.

However, that perfectly reasonable plan found itself in
jeopardy the instant a friend of Dad's had a sailboat for sale
(the aforementioned Mallard) and asked Dad if he was interested in buying it. Dad most definitely was; he was already getting into sailing by that point in his life, but he
didn't have a boat of his own to indulge his hobby with yet.
The deal looked really good too, so Dad did what any reasonable husband would do: he immediately picked up the
phone and called Mom to talk things over to see if there
were a way for them to afford the boat at that point in time.

HA! Just kidding! I had you going there for a second,
didn't I? What really happened was that Dad spent about 5
seconds (conservatively) thinking it over and decided to
take advantage of this amazing opportunity that had presented itself by using the money he and Mom were saving
for the carpet to purchase the sailboat.

Now, as a married man myself, I find myself unable to comprehend exactly how Dad could possibly have ever thought that was going to be a decision that any wife, let alone his, was going to just be OK with. And, I'd like to believe that my inability to figure out Dad's thinking on this has nothing to do with the benefit of hindsight; no matter how many ways I've thought about it, I've never been able to find a way to make the course of action Dad took look even remotely like a good idea. It just seems so obvious, like God in His wisdom hard-wired a kind of warning instinct into us against these kinds of things.

The truth is, though, that I seriously doubt that the thought that Mom wouldn't be "on board" with his purchase ever even entered into Dad's mind. So, when he showed up at home that day with a sailboat she had no idea was coming and had been purchased with the carpet money they'd been saving up, I am sure he was as surprised to see the look of wide-eyed horror on her face as she was about "their" new unplanned asset. It was always at such moments when it would finally dawn on Dad that there was something really important he hadn't fully considered; all you needed to do was to look at the expression on his face to know what he was thinking: "Uh, oh."

Thus, there was an evident innocence to the whole thing that characterized the person Dad was. It's sort of like when your child picks all of the flowers you just planted and gives them back to you as a gift. They get caught up in the joy of the vision of the moment and don't look at it like they just destroyed something you spent a lot of time and money on; they think they are doing something awesome and worthy of praise.

I think Dad's sailboat purchase was kind of like that child picking flowers. I believe he saw the sailboat as an opportunity to have something fun to do with his wife and family, a way to create a sense of close spaces and shared experiences. A way to make the most of the peace and quiet of a summer evening on the lake. A skill to master and pass onto his children. I think those ideas were the ones that captivated and inspired him, things that to him were so much more important than carpet.

I believe that there is such a thing as being right, but for the wrong reasons. Dad didn't make the smart call that day, but looking back now, I can see that he was at least onto something. Eventually, Mom and Dad did get carpet in the house, but we ultimately didn't end up staying there for very long after it went in. And to be perfectly honest, I don't really remember what life was like "B.C." (before carpet) or how life changed much after it went in. But the sailboat—I have many, many fond memories of sailing out on the water with Dad, of letting a warm July breeze take us to no place in particular, of falling asleep to the hypnotic slapping of waves against the hull as the day wore down. I will never forget those moments as long as I live, and I think they were among Dad's favorite moments in his life too.

Dad knew he screwed up that day and even named the boat after his folly, but I believe that his heart was in the right place even if he showed it in the wrong way. Sorry, Cutie.

———

To say that Mom and Dad had moved into a "fixer upper" was an understatement. Yet, Dad believed, it was necessary. All of the kids were married now, and keeping a
bigger house with a yard that needed hours of maintenance
each week didn't make much sense anymore. Dad was also
several years into cancer treatment by this point. While he
didn't know how much time he had left, he did know that it
would be good to downsize while he was still feeling good.
And, as an added bonus, they would be able to get rid of a
loan payment. It was just a matter of finding the right opportunity.

It turned that the "right opportunity" was when the
house right next door to my brother went up for sale. It was
the right size and the right price, and Dad knew that if his
health took a sudden turn for the worse, that he would have
family very close by to help Mom out through any emergency. But, the house had been built years ago and it
needed quite a bit of work. They fell in love with it, though,
and put an offer in despite the labor that would be needed
to get it into shape. The offer was accepted, and for the next
16 months, Dad put countless hours into making that old
house into their new home.

One of the major projects Dad had to work on was the
upstairs bathroom, and it was unfortunately no small task.
The previous owners had started a renovation in there, but
the work was shoddy and they weren't even close to finishing it. As a result, Dad had to tear what they had done
down and start over from scratch with an entirely new
plan.

At this point in Dad's life, he had only months left and
I suspect that, though he would never admit it, the cancer

he had fought for so long was taking a toll on his stamina. He started the project anyway, with the same energy and enthusiasm he put towards everything, determined to finish the bathroom "the right way."

It was messy, time consuming, and exhausting work, and throughout the project, Dad had his trusty shop vac with him the whole time to vacuum up all of the debris he was making. There was just one problem—the shop vac was rather large and there were not a lot of places where Dad could store it while it wasn't being used. Narrow hallways and rooms full of furniture and tools put space at a premium up there. Ultimately, Dad decided to put the shop vac in a corner near the top of the stairs that led down to the main floor, a location Mom was not particularly fond of. Often, she would express concern that she was going to trip over it and everything that was in it would tumble down the stairs. Dad's response was so typical—"C'mon, we're both adults! It'll be fine!"

It's easy to guess what happened next. Mom had just finished cleaning the floors downstairs and Dad, while working on the bathroom, accidentally bumped into the shop vac. Down it went, all the way down the stairs, spewing months of drywall dust, nails, and wood shavings all over the floor Mom had just cleaned. Mom, who was used to this sort of thing happening after 40 years of marriage, didn't say much—she just sighed and started cleaning up. Sorry, Cutie.

———

I never got to ask Dad why he didn't just listen to Mom in the first place and keep the shop vac out of "harm's way"; it seems like something that'd be as obvious as not buying a sailboat with carpet money. Maybe if I'd asked him he would have said, "I just wasn't thinking," and while I suspect that's true, I also don't believe that would be the whole truth. There was purpose behind everything Dad did. Even if I didn't necessarily agree with it or it wasn't obvious, it was always there.

So why leave a shop vac at the top of the stairs and not some place "safer"? Oddly, I think it may have been because he was thinking about my Mom. What if:

- Dad's strength was beginning to fade and he knew he'd need Mom, who was already carrying an exhaustive burden because of her job and his sickness, to help him move the shop vac safely night in and night out?

- He didn't want to waste precious time he knew was running out moving a silly shop vac around the upstairs when he could be finishing the projects he needed to in order to make the home perfect for Mom?

- Dad figured that, with a giant hole in the floor where the stairwell was with only a flimsy rail between him and the hole, if he tripped and fell moving the shop vac, the result would be the same as it falling down the stairs, only he was now running the risk of falling down the hole too, risking serious injury?

- That knowing all of this, he knew that if Mom knew he
  was thinking this way, that she would be way more worried about him than she already was?

Maybe some, or all, of those thoughts are wrong, but
what I do know is that when Dad said "Sorry, Cutie," there
was something deeper going on than just an apology towards Mom. Those words, offered only in the most "special" of circumstances, were an expression of something
far more profound—of humility, sincere but misguided intentions, and most importantly, love.

The funny thing is that with time, I think all of us in
my family now look at every "Sorry, Cutie" incident as a gift
rather than the "what the heck?" moments they seemed to
be when they happened. Not only has each one become a
life lesson for all of us, but they are an encouragement for
each of us to not be afraid to think differently, and are most
definitely the moments that we now laugh about the hardest when we talk amongst ourselves and to others about
Dad.

*"AND WE KNOW THAT IN ALL THINGS GOD
WORKS FOR THE GOOD OF THOSE WHO LOVE
HIM, WHO HAVE BEEN CALLED ACCORDING TO
HIS PURPOSE."*

– ROMANS 8:28

Portrait 6

I didn't intend to start writing this portrait of Dad until I found myself writing it. Today was a pretty long day —a very cool day, but the kind of day that when you get home, you just want to sit on the couch and not do a darned thing until it's time to turn in for the night. But that didn't happen. You see, I had a folder open on my computer when I got home. In that folder were a bunch of videos that were taken of services that our church held throughout the year in 2013.

I quickly scrolled down the list of videos and decided at random to play the file from April 14th, a day near Dad's birthday. It started up, and a few minutes into the video, there was Dad, standing up at his seat as the worship set was getting started. The song the band played was new to the church, but very upbeat, the kind of song that you just can't sit still during. Dad had this kind of bounce/sway thing going that made me laugh. Dad was never much of a dancer, but on this morning and on this song, Dad certainly was giving it his best shot!

On impulse, I decided to pull up the service from the previous week to see if Dad was there. He was, and in the same spot he was in service I'd just looked at. What about the week after April 14th? Yup, he was there too, again right in the same spot.

Finding Dad in those old videos didn't surprise me much, but it was a powerful reminder of how important the church was to Dad. And when I started thinking about it, thoughts and memories began to flood in that I knew I needed to start writing down.

Like many, Dad's spiritual journey started when he was a kid. Both of his parents were very Catholic, and they dutifully made sure their kids were brought up the same way, which meant Catechism and Sunday mass. In those days, I suspect Dad was like many others his age—you attend church and make your sacraments because your parents say so, and you DEFINITELY are aware of Hell and want to stay as far away from that business as possible. So, you try and live a fairly clean life—you're certainly no missionary, but you mostly try and do good in this world and treat people kindly.

And, that continues into adulthood. You decide you want to get married and your wife takes conversion classes so you *can* get married. You have a few kids, you get them baptized, and the cycle starts all over again. Right?

Not Dad. At some point in between having kids and the cycle starting all over again, something awakened in Dad that changed him for the rest of his life. He was introduced to a Jesus that was real and alive for the first time, and when Dad found him, nothing could be the same. Dad abandoned the faith of his youth and early adulthood in search of something else—the family switched over to a Lutheran church a few more miles down the road, Catechism gave way to Sunday School, and we were suddenly thrust into the world of the Protestants.

I don't remember very much about that church we switched to other than the name, but I remember that Dad was different—he talked about God more often, he started reading the Bible and other theology books, and he really made it his mission to try and live a God-honoring life. You could tell he had found a happiness he hadn't found before, and from that came a sense of total peace about the journey he was on.

After a few years at the new Lutheran church, the family moved to a different city an hour away. So, it was time to find a new place to spend Sunday mornings. Dad took on the responsibility for this, and I think most of us were grateful for that. We didn't have to sit through a bunch of bad services until we found the right church, and more importantly (for me, anyway), we could sleep in on Sundays during the search.

Dad found us a good place pretty quickly, though. The pastor was a good teacher, they had a robust kids program, and they did an excellent job with the worship music. They also rotated between different service liturgies so you got a mix of the old school green hymnal (not anyone's favorite) and more contemporary experiences. It was the perfect place for us—Mom and Dad joined the congregation, and soon we were all making friends and getting involved at the church.

One cool thing Mom and Dad did was volunteer as Sunday school teachers, which we kids really enjoyed because of the work they put into making it interesting and the fact that they were diligent about keeping the class under control. We also cleaned the church and did setup as a family every so often, which, as you can imagine, was not very popular among the younger members of the family. Personally, I am not sure what was worse for Mom and Dad —doing the actual work or listening to all of us (me, in particular) complain the whole time about having to serve. We did it anyway, though, because it was made clear to us that service was part of being part of a church. So, that's what we did.

Our time at this church was a period of intense spiritual growth for Dad. As Dad's life increasingly took on the character of God, people began to notice. Sometimes, they asked him why he was so different, so ... cheerful ... all the time. He would freely tell them about how God had touched his life, and on occasion, the conversation would go deeper. Other times, it didn't, and Dad would get a shrug or a weird look. When that happened, it didn't bother Dad in the least—he would still treat you as well as he possibly could whether you could stand it or not. He would listen without judging you, encourage you, and help you if he could. He would pray for you whether you were a friend or an enemy. He was the best kind of friend and an example of how to love people no matter where they were at in life and what they believed about God.

As an example of this, on occasion, Dad would encounter Jehovah's Witnesses showing up at the house, and instead of applying the usual technique of not answering the door or quickly bailing on the conversation, he used a different tactic. He enthusiastically welcomed the opening dialog to talk about God, but he would then get his Bible out and start lovingly correcting the flaws he saw in their doc- trine with scripture. Dad was incredibly smart, had done his homework, and had questions and responses for every- thing—they clearly were not used to meeting people like this!

The results were hilarious—some people would imme- diately start looking for an exit strategy and run for the hills as quickly as they could. Others, Dad would engage for incredibly long conversations, never giving an inch of ground. When asked why he'd "waste" so much time out- side in discussion with total strangers seemingly bent on "harassing" people, Dad would give a sly smile and answer, "I see this as a no-lose scenario. If I talk to them and they are convinced that maybe they need to take another look at things, it is a win for God. But, if after a long discussion, they are not convinced, I have sucked up so much of their time that they will be less able to try and do what they are doing to someone else." No matter what happened, though, there was another side benefit of Dad's activity—after a Je- hovah's Witness had gotten done talking with him, they started skipping over our house entirely when they were in the neighborhood.

At home, Dad's spirituality manifested itself in some ways that could be ... well ... kind of annoying at times. We all knew he meant well and that he took his role of family protector seriously, but he would complain incessantly about the TV shows we would watch, the music we'd listen to, and movies we'd rent. Sometimes, Dad would just walk up and turn something off if he didn't like what he saw or heard, a behavior he had learned from his dad. As you can imagine, though, this wasn't always (like ever) received very well, and as a result, there was often a bit of tension in the room when Dad was around and the TV or radio were on.

Looking back, I can say that Dad was right about some of it, and probably took some things that were not meant to be taken too seriously a bit too seriously. Thankfully, however, I think Dad realized after a few years that his good intentions were getting in the way of loving his family, and that to love someone meant that you had to let them make choices you didn't always agree with, talk through what is good and bad as best as you can, and let God sort out the rest. When Dad started doing that, he found that things seemed to work out a lot better (though he never was able to tolerate soap operas or *Wheel of Fortune*).

In the years that Dad's faith was maturing, there was a changing of the guard at pastor at the new church, something none of us had experienced before. I remember being a little shaken up about it too. Yes, the current pastor had said that he'd felt a strong call from God to go to this new place and that should have been of some comfort in accepting the situation, but it really wasn't. You start to develop unhealthy questions like "Why would God call this guy we liked away from us?" and "What do we do if God 'calls' someone to this church and we don't like him?"

We also all quickly realized that a church in transition is a very difficult place to be at. You need a leader, someone setting the priorities and direction for the congregation. You can't do that when you are subbing guest pastors in and out each week. You don't maintain any continuity and people start to feel disconnected from the church. The longer this goes on, the worse it gets, and it seemed like it took an awfully long time to find a new pastor for our congregation.

We stuck with it, though, and the church eventually did find a new pastor. His arrival was an incredible relief for everyone—not only did he provide some much needed stability, but he didn't radically change too much about the way the church ran, preferring instead to make incremental improvements over time. Plus, his family was great—very kind, very supportive, and extremely talented musically, which made the worship music all the more enjoyable.

I can see now, though, that the period of transition we'd endured had begun to form cracks in our family's relationship with the church. While the new pastor was settling in with his new constituency about as well as anyone could imagine, he did suffer from a fatal flaw that wasn't at all his fault—he wasn't the other guy.

In his heart, I know that Dad sincerely wanted things to work out with the new pastor. He obviously had known that things wouldn't be exactly the same, but there were some doctrinal things that they just didn't agree on. When I first found out about this, I was kind of shocked—I didn't think it was "allowed" to disagree with your pastor! I sincerely believed this was one of those things that would land you an eternity in the darkest pits of Hell.

But, I also knew two things about Dad—that there was no doubt he was not going to Hell and that he was very well studied in scripture. He talked to us about some of the things he disagreed with and showed us Bible passages that explained why he disagreed. He also told us that the pastor was a good person, to keep listening to the good things he had to say, and that it was fine to attend a place where you don't agree with everything that's said from the pulpit.

This always bothered me, however, and I wouldn't be surprised if it bothered others in the family at least a little bit as well. As I grew older and got into confirmation classes, the discontent I personally was experiencing with the church increased dramatically. The classes I had to attend in order to get "confirmed" were led by the pastor and I can truly say I hated them for a wide number of reasons. I began to wonder quite earnestly what the point of some of the things we were doing was. I also began to question if there were any things that the pastor was saying in class that Dad wouldn't agree with. Being around thirteen at the time, subtlety wasn't exactly my specialty and I made sure *everyone* knew how unhappy I was with the things I was experiencing.

Dad was incredibly kind and helpful to me during this time in my life, continuing to affirm in me things that needed to be affirmed and helping me to find a way to keep pressing on every week. And, it turned out that there were things going on that he wasn't fully on board with either. But, I think he was sensing something deeper—a growing feeling that the church was no longer meeting our needs as a family.

One key sign was that the reasons we came up with for deciding to skip church kept increasing. Some weeks we skipped because they were using the dreaded green hymnals in the service. In other weeks, we skipped because we found other things to do on Sunday mornings. Other times, we had gotten home just a little too late on Saturday night to get up for church.

Dad tried to fill in the gaps in our church attendance as best he could because he knew it was important. One tactic he tried for a while was taping Robert Schuller's *Hour of Power* and having us all watch it together and discuss. In time, however, we stopped doing even that, and we became one of "those families" that only attended church on Christmas and Easter.

I know it bothered Dad that we were not attending church regularly anymore as a family or otherwise, but I think he struggled with a solution. Dad told me later in his life that he regretted not acting on the warning signs sooner, but we had all kind of reached a point where we professed a belief in God but at the same time, a complete dislike of attending church. Further, we were now old enough to make our own decisions about what we would and would not do. I am sure Dad spent a lot of time praying about this dilemma, but the reality was that it was going to take a miracle to get most of us back into a sanctuary on any sort of regular basis.

Thankfully, though, God's in the miracle business, and He started weaving together a story only He could put together. The son of a family friend had experienced a radical transformation from atheist/agnostic to accepting the gospel, and he had quit his steady job as an engineer as a result. If that weren't enough, he was heading to seminary in California to become a pastor. He enthusiastically told Dad about this nondenominational church he was attending that had inspired all of this to take place. What he described sounded like a completely different church experience, one that Dad had hoped would resonate with everyone. Dad went to a service to check things out and was hooked immediately—here was a church that had awesome teaching, outstanding leadership, and worked incredibly hard to engage people who had given up on church through music, drama, media, etc.

Dad came home from the service and excitedly told the rest of us about it. He was emphatic that we all check it out with him, and while we took him up on the offer, by that time we were beginning to head in our own directions as individuals. For example, the woman who would become my wife and I were already heading the direction of attending a different church. Everyone else had different relationship statuses and priorities.

And so, while Dad had found a reason to go back to church again, he was going pretty much by himself every week. But, he wasn't "alone," not for very long anyway. Dad soon developed friendships with others at the church by joining a men's small group and by helping out one of the lead pastors. The story of how the latter relationship developed is kind of a fun story—Dad had heard this pastor talk a few times about how he wasn't good around the house, and after one service, Dad went up to him and offered to give him a hand with whatever he needed. The offer was accepted, and Dad showed up at the appointed time ready to get to work and with a box of candy for the pastor's family. The pastor thought he'd hit the jackpot! However, when Dad's decision to not shut off the water while working on the plumbing resulted in water spraying all over the place, I can imagine that the term "hitting the jackpot" was not what was on the pastor's mind.

It was one of those awkward moments that I can't imagine I'd know what to do with, but Dad's reaction was to laugh, and laugh incredibly hard at the situation. And, the pastor, feeling the contagious nature of Dad's laughter, laughed right along with him. More importantly, however, a powerful relationship was formed that day, one characterized by brotherhood, fellowship, and encouragement. Over the years, these two men would spend hours together sharing a meal or fixing something in the pastor's home, all while discussing everything under the sun from family life to spiritual matters.

Dad also managed to keep in touch with the still in school pastor-in-training who had brought him to his new church home. Dad was very interested in what he was learning and would occasionally check in to see how things were going. This was often done via email, but they were also able to meet up for lunch during times where they were both in town. After a few years, when his school was done, this family friend returned home and landed a job at the place that had given both of them a fresh start with church.

Time continued to pass and Dad went his own way spiritually while the rest of us went our own way. My older sister had married a man who was part of the Catholic church, so that's where she landed. When my younger siblings decided to get married, Dad arranged for the family friend to officiate their weddings, but that was about as far as things got church-wise.

I personally found myself quitting on the church again after a pastor I had really liked left the place that we were attending to start a new community that was too far away for us to attend. After that happened, I couldn't help but

feel a sense of déjà vu that recalled a past that I wasn't particularly interested in repeating. So, I ended up withdraw-
ing my interest in attending church entirely for a while.
Dad was concerned and he often told me so. I kept telling
him I'd go back "someday," but in my heart I really didn't
know when that might be.

In November of 2009, I got an email from Dad regarding that son of the family friend who'd decided to become a
pastor. He was really sick with a severe infection in his
chest cavity and needed urgent prayers. It was a scary situation, but this email was the first that made me really start
to pay attention to the things that were going on in this
young pastor's life. He recovered, and then I forgot about
him for a few months until I received another email from
Dad in April of 2010 about a series of sermons the pastor
was doing at a church in the area on Thursday nights. A
few weeks later, during the period of time where he was
processing through being diagnosed with cancer, Dad told
me that the pastor was going to be launching a church of
his own soon, and asked if I'd be willing to help him with
their website.

One thing quickly led to another and my wife and kids
plus Dad ended up deciding to join the newly started
church. Something that had really attracted us beyond
solid Biblical teaching was the pastor's stated goal for
church members to have an experience with God every
Sunday—to see Him actively working in our lives, to use
His Power to bring the Kingdom of Heaven to a fallen
world, and to feel His amazing love for His children. He
taught that these experiences were available to us because
God is good, all the time. The emphasis on these things was

new to us, and were a weekly call to live lives that were counter to how the culture said to live.

The church also put an incredibly heavy emphasis on the power of prayer, having prayer teams available after every service for people who needed it. Dad went up for prayer often, and not only did he see breakthroughs in his life happen, he was filled with constant joy and was more keenly aware of God's presence in his life than he'd ever been. In his time as a cancer patient, it would have been easy for Dad to slip into depression and anxiety like many other people with a similar prognosis do, but Dad seemed completely oblivious to the "norm." He was grateful, blessed, energetic, and had an insatiable appetite for life— so much so that at Dad's memorial service, my uncle hilari-ously relayed a story about Dad that included the phrase, "Did someone forget to tell him that he has cancer?"

In the end, the church ended up being the perfect place for Dad during the battle for his life; the timing literally could not have been better. There are some who would at-tribute this to just a coincidence, but I don't fully subscribe to that theory. It seems to me that it is fully within God's power to take Dad's story and interweave it into a whole lot of other people's in order to create something they all need. So, while I don't necessarily believe that all of this came to-gether "just for Dad," I do believe that God had Dad and the community who was going to be part of it in mind when this church was being planted

One night in late September, a few weeks before he died, Dad called me on the phone. He told me he was feel-ing weak, was battling a virus of some sort, and was in a lot of pain. He knew we prayed as a family every night, and he asked if we would pray for him over the phone. I gathered up the family and that's what we did, praying for restoration and for his strength to return. The next day we received the following email from Dad:

> *Just want you to know that since you prayed for me last night, have been feeling 100% better. Best day in 4 weeks!! Cold gone, appetite back, not hurting all over or feeling blah. Thanks for being there for me yesterday and every day. Prayer works!*

We didn't stop praying for Dad, and for several weeks after that night, he seemed to be doing pretty well. But, it wasn't long before things got very serious with Dad's health and he ended up in the hospital due to incredible and overwhelming pain. The church rallied prayers and support, and our pastor visited him at his room in the hospital to encourage and pray for him. One time, after receiving prayer, Dad started talking in a voice barely louder than a whisper. At first, the pastor thought he was thanking him for coming or that Dad was babbling because of the pain medications Dad was on. But, it wasn't either of those. Dad was actually doing something I later found out he did whenever he'd received prayer; after he had received, he gave back by saying prayers for the person who had prayed for him. Dad, barely coherent and dying of cancer, was praying for our pastor and his family.

On the day after he first entered the hospital, I was sitting with Dad as he slipped in and out of consciousness. A doctor came into the room to talk to him about his condition, and Dad very sleepily introduced me, saying, "This is my son. I am so proud of him. He is such a man of God."

In that moment, I thought about the life Dad had led and how it had served as such a positive example for his family. I thought about people whose lives he'd touched because of his love for God. I remembered Dad's commitment to serving others. And, then I thought about the verse in the Bible that talks about the Son only being able to do what he sees his Father doing (John 5:19) and looked over at Dad.

"No," I said silently, "you are."

Portrait 7

THE kids are across the room huddled up with Dad, talking in hurried but hushed tones, their little round faces lit up with excitement. After another minute or so, the conversation breaks up and our kids make a beeline towards my wife and I to ask a question we both know was coming—the look on Dad's face and the heat of the summer had already given it away.

"Dad, dad!" they say, "Can we go get ice cream with Papoh?"

I look at my wife and she is already nodding her assent. "Of course you can go get ice cream with Papoh," I say. The kids make a happy noise and scamper off to get their shoes on. I go over to Dad and whisper, "You know, we weren't really going to tell them 'no', right?"

Dad smiles, "I did, but I think it's important for them to see that they always need to ask Mom and Dad first."

"You're probably right about that," I answer. "Hopefully they see that if you need to get permission from us, they will realize they need to as well."

"Exactly," says Dad.

The kids are ready to go. "Let's go, Papoh!" they exclaim, already tugging on his arm to get him out the door..

Dad gives me a knowing wink and they are they are off. "Have fun with Papoh!" I call after them, even though I know it isn't necessary. Dad was taking his grandkids out for ice cream—they were guaranteed a great time!

———

Dad—"Papoh"—cherished every moment he spent with his four grandchildren. He treated each child as a special gift, each one acting just like their parents in some ways but also their own people in so many others. He not only played with them, but he spent countless hours of time talking with them about what they wanted to talk about and listening—always listening—to what the smallest amongst us had to say.

In Matthew 19:14, Jesus said "Let the little children come to me, and do not hinder them, for the kingdom of heaven belongs to such as these." This one was of Dad's favorite verses in the Bible—he knew that kids have a lot to teach adults about life, about joy, and about things that are *really* important. In his grandchildren, Dad found some of the best teachers ever to help him with living in the world with child-like eyes and wonder.

His first grandchild happened to be my wife and I's first child, a daughter with pretty brown eyes and infectious enthusiasm. She has an active imagination and was constantly in motion for many years, always wanting to try new things and introducing herself to everyone she met. if she wanted to play with you, it didn't particularly matter what you had going on—she would pull you in through the sheer force of her innocence and personality, leaving you with no choice but to go along with it.

As she developed an affinity for reading and playing video games in her toddler years, she would come up to you with a book she wanted you to read to her or grab your hand to drag you over to the desk where the computer was. Dad was a frequent target for these "attacks" because the word "no" shouldn't be in a grandparent's vocabulary when it came to stuff like that. And so, he would sit and read whatever stories she wanted to read with her, and always listened carefully while she explained a particular game to him and what she was doing in it. Dad loved the interaction —he paid attention to everything she said, and was always asking her follow-up questions about the things she said so she knew he was paying attention.

After spending time with her, Dad would always talk about how sweet and pure of heart she was, and I believe these were the qualities he admired most in her.

It was this grandchild who came up with the nickname "Papoh" for Dad, which was a twisting of the name "grandpa." When her brother was born a few years later, he adopted the name just as soon as he learned to talk, and it stuck.

Her brother, by the way, was Dad's second grandchild, and he was born several years after his older sister. Dad was extremely excited and a little anxious about his birth because we'd found out that he only had one kidney, and thus my requests to not contact us while we were in surgery waiting for him to be delivered via C-section ended up being completely ignored. My intention was to try and avoid having to respond to a million messages when we tiredly returned to the birthing suite, but when we did and I looked down at my phone, I saw that Dad had sent several asking for an update, despite the fact that he knew we were stuck in the operating room.

Anyhow, with our son's arrival, Dad got to experience grandparenthood in a whole new way—now there were two kids to keep busy, each with their own personalities and interests. For example, our son showed an early interest in building things that his sister didn't really share. Dad noticed it though, and would often ask him if he wanted to go to the building supply store with him to pick up tools or building materials. The answer was always yes, and I think Dad was happy to have the company along for the ride. When they would return, they'd both set to work until the task before them was complete. They would then often share a treat together in celebration of a job well done.

Dad also found that he and his grandson enjoyed cooking together. One of my favorite memories in this vein was the time Dad took our son home from church one day, and he convinced his grandparents to make these apple dumplings he had recently seen on TV cooking show. When Dad reached for a recipe book, however, he was quickly stopped by a child determined to not *just* make apple dumplings, but the *exact* apple dumplings he had seen a few nights before. It took Mom quite a while to find the recipe, but it was eventually located, allowing baking to finally commence. When they were done and our son arrived home, they were proudly presented to us for sampling, and I have to admit that the results were very tasty.

Just about two years after Dad's second grandchild was born, another new bundle of joy arrived. This time, it was my older sister and her husband with the special delivery, and they were blessed with the arrival of a daughter. As she grew up, Dad got to see her quite often—nearly daily— because of how her parents' schedules were and the fact that Mom took her to their house after school every day.

There are some little girls who radiate charisma and sunshine, and she is definitely cut from that cloth. Every time I saw her arrive at Mom and Dad's house after a long day in the classroom, she was full of hugs and smiles. Dad would often greet her with his favorite question: "What was the best thing that happened to you today?" She would tell him, he would say something grandfatherly, and then she'd be off to play or get her homework done.

Being the bright and observant kid she is, she noticed that our kids called Dad "Papoh" and she started calling him that too, with a little "grandpa" mixed in for good measure. But, when all three grandkids were together, inevitably, "Papoh" was the name that won out over anything else.

Dad would have to wait just over five more years after she was born for his last grandchild, a boy born to my brother and his wife, to arrive. And when we got to see that newborn face for the first time, it was a lift in the spirits I think we all needed. By that time, Dad had been diagnosed with cancer, so being able to celebrate the birth of a new baby was a welcome respite from some of the weightiness of Dad's illness.

Shortly after he was born, Mom and Dad ended up moving into the house right next door to him. A huge advantage to this was that their new home had a pretty awesome playscape in the back yard. Often, when I would stop by to visit, Dad would be in the back yard with him, watching him go on the swings or slide down the slide. In those moments, it was hard to tell who was enjoying the time more—Dad or his youngest grandson.

He called Dad "Pupah" when he learned to talk, which I figure was close enough to "Papoh" that you could say that all of his grandchildren knew him by his nickname. I don't know if Dad preferred it that way or not, but in a way, I did. When I thought of the name "grandpa," I thought of my own grandfathers, who we only saw a handful of times per year as children, if at all. It wasn't that they were mean or distant or anything like that—it was just that they lived in different states and could only visit every so often.

I am so glad, though, that all of Dad's grandkids had a much different experience than we did, that they have more than fleeting memories of Dad at holidays or family reunions. Dad was familiar to all of them, and because he was, I always felt he was deserving of a name that transcended the formal in favor of something that implied a closer relationship. "Papoh," rather than a name being given to him, became a name he earned. And he did so in many, many different ways.

The first way was by always treating the grandkids like they mattered to him. Dad would often drop what he was doing to listen to them tell a story, go play, or fix the occasional snack. Whatever he was eating at the time, he offered to share with them, even if it was kind of gross looking. He invited them to sit with him on the couch during movie time. He took them on tractor rides. He shared family wisdom and insights with them, and told funny stories about their parents. And, he told them constantly that they were loved, never letting them say goodbye without a hug.

Dad was also known for coming up with ideas to bring the kids together and have fun. Sometimes it was going out for a treat, especially to my brother's candy shop. Other times it was going outside to kick a ball around. Still other activities … well … he certainly had fantastic intentions, but sometimes thing went a little awry. Let me explain.

I think one of the reasons Dad related to the grandkids so well was because he often thought like they did. At times, this served him very well, but at others, it had a tendency to get him into trouble. Like the time he was playing outside with the kids and they were involved in some sort of tag/hide and seek game in a yard that he "kind of" knew was full of poison ivy. But, since he was caught up in the game, he wasn't paying that close of attention. Luckily, though, he remembered, quickly fessed up, and due to a fast trip to the pharmacy for some special soap and a quick immersion in the bathtub, the kids avoided getting a rash. However, the timing of all of this was what was most hilarious—all of this took place at my brother and wife-to-be's bridal shower.

There was also the time when we were down in Ohio for my cousin's wedding and Dad had a massive craving for ice cream from a nearby place that he was very fond of. I'm not sure what he was thinking, but he decided that the best time to go there was right before the wedding, naively (and *very* wrongly) thinking the kids wouldn't make a mess of their nice clothes. I'm not sure, actually, if the stains ever did come out.

No, sometimes Dad would show all of the common sense of a person less full of years...

At other times, Dad could be incredibly thoughtful with the kids. A couple of times, Dad had our son spend the night so they could do "man stuff" together. Sometimes, they went fishing with a friend or they worked on a big project, but other times, it was just because Dad wanted to share a few meals with a son from the next generation. Either way, he created memories that will be around for a very, very long time.

Finally, Dad made himself available for things that the kids participated in. He was there for dance and gymnastics recitals, ball games, band concerts, you name it. He loved seeing the talents of his grandchildren on display, and you could tell by the smile on his face while the performance was going on that being there meant more to him than anything. When the kids were released back to their families at the end of the night, he would always talk to the kids about how great they did and how proud of them he was.

Dad made every effort to attend as many of these events as he could for his grandkids, but it became harder and harder for him to do so in his final months of life be-

Connection Card

THE MISSION

- ☐ "This is my first time here."
- ☐ "I've attended a few times."
- ☐ "I attend regularly."

Name: _____ Phone: _____

Email: _____

Address: ☐ Change of Address

_____ ZIP: _____

Prayer Request: _____

_____

_____

(please use the back side if you need more room)   (6/23/2019)

MY ACTION STEP TODAY:
- ☐ Reflect on 2 Corinthians 12:7
- ☐ I am going to read one of the Suggested Resources.
- ☐ I am going to go through the Digging Deeper Questions, either by myself or with a friend!
- ☐ I'd like more information about donating to or volunteering at Samaritan House.
- ☐ I'd like to attend the Cleaning Crew Volunteer Lunch on June 30th.

_____

_____

_____

_____

I WANT MORE INFO ABOUT:
- ☐ Vineyard National Conference
- ☐ Stephen Ministry
- ☐ Fire on Fridays
- ☐ Volunteering at Samaritan House
- ☐ Becoming a CR Leader

I'D LIKE TO VOLUNTEER IN:
- ☐ ProPresenter (slides)
- ☐ Mission Kids
- ☐ Security
- ☐ Café
- ☐ Camera
- ☐ Usher/Greeter
- ☐ Cleaning Crew

cause the cancer had made his body so weak. As a result, there was one class of event that Dad simply wasn't able to get to—our daughter's football game marching band performances. She was a freshman at a brand new school that year, and he had heard from us how awesome the show they put on at half time was. He wanted to go to at least one game, but he couldn't find the strength to make the fairly long trip out and back and sit outside for two to three hours. We all understood and showed him pictures and videos instead, but there is something about "being there" that I know Dad wanted to experience for himself.

Interestingly, as the season progressed, there ended up being a contest on the schedule that provided Dad with the opportunity he'd been looking for: the team was scheduled to play an away game at a high school just a few minutes away from Mom and Dad's house. Normally, the band doesn't travel with the football team, but this was a special case. The band directors from both schools had an established tradition of bringing the bands together for the game to perform, fundraise, and raise awareness around a special cause. More importantly, this put Dad's wish to see his eldest granddaughter perform with the marching band within reach! And so, Mom and Dad made plans to go.

The night of the game ended up being a bit rainy, but the bad weather went away just before kickoff, allowing Dad to join everyone in the stands. He loved both the game (our team won by a mile) and the band performance, and our daughter's face was radiant when she saw that Dad had been able to make it.

That night turned out to be the first and only time Dad got to see her perform with the marching band. It was an extraordinary night for everyone, full of clapping, high fives, and giant grins. Oh, and the special cause that had made this all possible? It was to recognize families affected by cancer. Coincidence? Maybe, but in my heart I truly believe that God was working a little miracle out for Dad on that particular October evening.

But, that wasn't the only miracle Dad was experiencing related to his grandkids around that time. I mentioned earlier that Dad had four grandchildren. This is mostly true, but it is not the whole story. Through the years, there were some fertility struggles and miscarriages the family had faced. However, by the time Dad passed away, he knew that he had not one, but two, new grandchildren on the way, both born a few months after Dad died and within a day of one another. Both are precious little girls—I know Dad would have been smitten the moment he saw them were he still with us.

There were a few people at Dad's visitation/funeral who lamented that Dad wouldn't get an opportunity to see the new additions to the family, but we all knew he'd be watching them grow up from afar. At the same time, something even more encouraging entered into my thoughts—that there were unborn grandchildren in Heaven who Dad was finally getting to meet for the very first time. I am certain it was a joyous reunion for Dad—I can just see him hugging them, telling them how much he loves them, and proudly telling stories about the ones he left behind. As hard as it was to lose Dad, getting a picture like that in my head was a powerful antidote to the sadness surrounding the loss of his life.

Still, there was the unfortunate reality that we as parents had to explain to our kids why Papoh wasn't going to be around anymore. They were not surprised by the news —they all knew he had cancer, and they all knew that he was very sick when he entered the hospital. There were tears shed, but there were encouraging words from all of the kids. Both of ours shared with us how they knew they would see Papoh again someday, and my sister's daughter expressed similar sentiments. But, perhaps the most profound wisdom came from Dad's three year old grandson.

"It's OK, dad," he told my brother, "Pupah is always going to be with us."

When that was shared with me, I thought about the amazing memories he'd made with all of the grandkids and the legacy he'd left for all of us as both father and grandfather. I looked around at all of the little faces and what features and personality traits they'd gotten from Dad through all of us. My little nephew was right—"Papoh," while we could no longer see him, was still with us, and would always be.

Portrait 8

I N Chapter 21 of the Book of John in the New Testament, there is a story about Peter and some of the disciples going out fishing all night and not catching a
thing. Jesus shows up in the morning, telling them to try
again and a miracle happens—their nets were full!

I feel like that story about the disciples is a pretty good
metaphor for Dad's experience as a fisherman—not catching anything and hoping for a miracle.

The fact of the matter is that Dad really enjoyed fishing, particularly with his family and friends. He started at
a pretty young age with the hobby, spending many afternoons and evenings on a small nearby lake honing his
skills, often with his younger brother in tow. During those
years, Dad managed to procure all kinds of fishing gear—
several rods and reels, as well as a cornucopia of fishing
lures that he stuffed into a large, ancient-looking tackle
box.

This is the gear we boys fished with when we were old enough to start going on Lake Huron with Dad. That, or we used one of those short Snoopy fishing rods that were incredibly popular back in the 1980s. I actually remember strongly preferring the Snoopy rods—some of the stuff Dad had hung onto looked like it should have been discarded long ago, and my brother and I were convinced that such dilapidated gear didn't stand a chance of catching anything.

Though we fished for all kinds of different species over the years, when we went fishing, it was typically for either walleye or perch—two of Dad's favorite kinds of freshwater fish to eat. Catching the former type of fish required drifting for about a mile north of the area where Lake Huron drains into the St. Clair River either very early in the morning or in the evening. The latter required anchoring out near the shipping channel, and Dad always said it didn't matter what time of the day we went out for them. However, when we fished for perch, we would usually fish during the day.

I personally preferred fishing for yellow perch, mostly because we usually didn't have to get up too early to go fishing, we could keep any size perch we caught (unlike walleye, where the notion of a "keeper" was introduced), and because I can remember that we had once had a fishing trip for the fish (that oddly took place on a sailboat) that was uncharacteristically successful. Though my memory of the day is pretty fuzzy because of my age when it happened, I do recall us pulling perch into the boat two at a time. I figured that if something like that had happened once, it could happen again.

Dad, on the other hand, seemed to prefer walleye fishing to perch fishing. I think he liked that they were harder to catch and that they put up more of a fight than perch did. Plus, there was something about getting up early or staying out late with his sons that Dad never seemed to get tired of.

I'd like to think it was those memories that kept Dad going back out with us summer after summer because it sure was never the quality of the fishing. While we all enjoyed one another's company and spending time out on the lake, the truth is that we were often quite a debacle when we headed out for a fishing trip, rarely coming back with anything. I know this frustrated Dad a bit—he was good at a ton of things, but there was a code to fishing which he never could seem to crack. There was also the reality that when he fished, he had a significant handicap—my brother and me.

If you ever fish with young children, you will notice that they tend to do a number of highly annoying and unproductive things while fishing, and we were no exception to that rule. When we had our lines in the water for perch, we were always calling Dad over to make sure we were on the lake bottom (despite the fact that the boat wasn't moving) and were not particularly adept at telling when a fish was nibbling on the bait. There were more "false alarms" that I can count, and equally frustrating, quite the number of times where we'd ignored a sudden tug on the line for too long and our bait had been eaten, causing Dad to have to stop what he was doing and help us "reload."

Walleye fishing, though, was a special kind of torture for Dad. First, both of us absolutely refused to bait worms —minnows, we could do, but I in particular lacked the conviction necessary to get one of those extremely slimy little buggers onto a hook. The other problem was that, due to the drifting we did, our lines were constantly getting snagged on seaweed and other debris on the lake bottom. Suffice it to say, Dad was constantly trying to get us untangled, or more likely, re-rigging the fishing pole because the snag was so bad that the line snapped and we lost the hook and lure entirely. This literally happened to us dozens of times—we lost a lot of good fishing tackle to the depths of Lake Huron.

Dad also had to deal with the human—errr... child—element of going out fishing with us. Complaints about being too hot or bored or that we were getting bit by flies were all too common. We also thought that yelling "here fishy, fishy, fishy" into the water as we'd seen Ernie do on *Sesame Street* (seriously, Google "Bert and Ernie Fish Call" if you don't believe me that this is a real thing) would help for reasons I cannot possibly fathom. We even managed to get our fishing lines caught in trees that were adjacent to the driveway because we wanted to practice our casting techniques from shore.

Rather than be overly discouraged by all of this, Dad found a way, as he often did, to fuel his own creative problem solving ability. Lures that were lost were quickly replaced by new ones we all would make with materials Dad bought from the fishing store. Dad worked on the snagging problem by finding these really neat sinkers that were supposed to prevent lines from getting tangled up with stuff at the bottom of the lake (which we managed to get tangled anyway). He started a contest where we would win money for things like catching the first fish, catching the biggest fish, and catching the most fish so we stopped complaining about being bored. He talked to other fishermen in the area about where to fish, and was always looking for good ideas. We never really got any better at fishing, but we had a lot of fun trying different things to see if they would help our horrible luck!

Those years were fun, but in time, my brother and I grew older and there just wasn't as much time to go fishing anymore. I am sure this saddened Dad a little bit, but we all had our own goals and life priorities which we were trying to keep in balance. Making time for something we were never really good at anyway didn't seem to make a whole lot of sense.

Dad, however, never really gave up on his interest in fishing. Instead, he was just biding his time until he got a grandson who was old enough for him to start all over again with. When my wife's and my son was born a few years into our marriage, Dad seized the opportunity, getting him a fishing pole and having him tag along for a night out on the lake with his brother and two boys just as soon as he was old enough.

What was really cool was that Dad was so good about fueling our son's passion for fishing. Dad would take him to the bait store to buy worms or minnows, and they'd talk with the owner about where the fishing was best. When they returned, he would let his grandson share all the things they'd heard from the "experts" while Dad would proudly nod his approval that the newest fisherman amongst us had gotten every detail right.

Dad also taught him about all of the tackle in his tackle box, which resulted in our son constantly wanting to switch things out when we inevitably weren't catching anything. Dad was a good sport about it, and often obliged, even though he knew trying to catch yellow perch with a casting rig was pointless. It was way more important to Dad that the little guy have fun and enjoy the experience of being out on the water.

In the summer of 2013, while my wife and daughter were out of town, Dad, my son (who had just turned nine), and I decided to spend a week together up at my parents' house on the lake. We decided to call it "male week," and the goal was just to spend time bonding and doing stuff to-gether. It was awesome—we played baseball, we ate bar-beque every night (at my son's request), and we spent a great deal of time out on the water fishing.

On the first day we went out, we decided to make an adventure of the day and head about 35 miles north of where the boat was stored to a spot Dad had received a "hot tip" about when he went to get bait. It took a while for us to get up there, and when we arrived, we puttered around for what seemed like hours trying to find a good place to set the anchor. We eventually found a spot that looked promising, baited our hooks, and set to fishing.

To our complete shock, Dad had a fish on his hook al-most immediately, and he reeled it in, much to the delight of his grandson. However, delight quickly turned to disap-pointment when we realized what Dad had caught—a goby, which is an invasive type of fish and not useful for any-thing else but plant fertilizer. In fact, the fish are so disrup-tive to the ecosystem in our area that the DNR requests that people who catch them make sure they don't end up getting thrown back into the lake, if you catch my "drift."

As irritating as that was, we soon experienced something that was far worse. It turns out the gobies have very small mouths and will eat at your bait without getting hooked. So, you'll feel a nibble on your line, attempt to set your hook, reel in, and discover that your bait is gone. This probably happened to us about 30 times that day, with my son being the primary target for having this happen.

In the end, while the day was quite nice, we didn't catch a thing that day and we headed back to shore. Dad and I felt a familiar sense of discouragement, but thankfully, the youngest member of our group wasn't fazed in the slightest! He was adamant that we head out and try again the next day, and so that's what we did.

We decided, however, to try some fishing spots that were a little closer to home instead of spending so much time trying to get to a place so far up the lake. This turned out to be a pretty good decision—we found a place we liked, got set up, and it wasn't long before Dad was once again the first person to catch a fish. Excited to finally make some progress, we fished on, and I eventually got one on my hook. I reeled it in, got it close to the boat, and Dad got the net out to bring it aboard. For some reason, though, Dad ended up fiddling with the net for what seemed like forever, and managed to find a way to knock the fish loose while he was trying to scoop it up. It was a bit of a frustrating moment, but we all laughed it off—accidents happen right?

We ended the day getting just a couple of fish (all caught by Dad), but we were all encouraged by the trip—at least we were not empty handed this time. So, we set out again the next day, hitting the same spot that had been successful for us the day before. This time, instead of Dad, I was the one who landed the first fish, and as I reeled it in, Dad once again got the net ready. As it got close to the boat, Dad was overwhelmed by the same malaise he had experienced the day before and proceeded to knock the fish off the hook again.

This time, I couldn't laugh it off so easily, and both my son and I decided right then and there that Dad was no longer going to be the guy in charge of working the net. It ended up not mattering much in the end—we didn't catch anything else that day.

When we got back on shore, Dad resolved that he was not going to let his grandson suffer the same fishing disappointments we'd all experienced in our younger years. He promised him that we'd all go out on a fishing charter as soon as we could, and in the meantime, he contacted our pastor's father, who was not only a family friend, but an excellent fisherman. Dad arranged for the three of them to head out on a little excursion early one morning, and they had a blast—we even got a video of the highlights of the trip that brings a smile to my face every time we watch it.

The promised outing with a fishing charter took just about another year to get arranged, but plans were eventually set in place to head out in the middle of the summer of 2014. Dad and my uncle decided to go through a guy they had been out with in the past, and they knew it would be a great time. He also guaranteed results, so we knew we were in the best possible hands. The only problem was the weather...

When our scheduled day originally came up, the captain of the boat called us in the morning to say that there was no way we would be able to get out of the harbor where the boat was stored—the lake was way too rough and it was very cold. We quickly rescheduled, and the day of the second try looked quite promising as we made the long trip up to the city the charter fished out of. However, by the time we arrived, the wind had picked up significantly, and it was again way too windy and choppy to go out. We turned around and headed home, all of us disappointed that we'd been foiled again. The guy who ran the boat even told all of us that having to reschedule a group twice in the same year was unheard of. It seemed that our bad luck with fishing was even carrying over to our plans to go out with our hired expert.

We rescheduled one more time for the last day that the boat would be doing trips out on our side of the state for 2014—if we didn't get out that day, it'd be a long 12 months of waiting before we'd be able to give it another shot, which none of us wanted to do. We anxiously watched the forecast in the days leading up to the scheduled date of our third attempt, and it wasn't looking good. While the forecast called for some sun, it also called for high winds, and we knew the wind would make rough seas that would more than likely keep us on shore again.

When the day finally arrived, we talked to the captain of the boat around noon and he told us he'd been holed up for several days, and also that he had to cancel the trip that was on his calendar for that morning already. We were scheduled to head out at 2:30 PM, but he put the odds at about 50-50 that the trip would have to be canceled yet a third time. Having nothing to lose, we decided that we would at least give it a try, so we got in the car and headed up the lake again. None of us were particularly optimistic about our chances, but that's when something very interesting happened.

In the Gospels, there are several accounts of Jesus calming a storm, and since we were well aware of that story, it ended up becoming the prayer for the trip up. I even had a few of my good friends who were aware of our frustrations with having to reschedule pray for the weather to cooperate. It seems those prayers were heard because by the time we were set to the leave the dock, the wind had died down and the waves had almost completely flattened out. Our fishing guide couldn't believe it—he even said, without any prompting from us, that he had never seen the weather calm down like that so fast in all his many years on the lake. Dad and I shared a look in that moment—something very cool had just happened!

And so, we headed out into the lake and proceeded to have the time of our lives. We all took turns reeling fish into the boat, and it was both exhilarating and exhausting. There were so many over-the-top awesome moments in the hours we spent out there; I had never done anything like that in my life, and catching fish like that was a thrill. My son ended up catching the biggest fish of the day, and I managed to take a video of him and Dad reeling it in together as grandfather and grandson. There were giant smiles on everyone's faces, and we ultimately landed 8 medium to large lake trout, 3 walleyes, 2 pink salmon, and a few bass that we ended up throwing back. It was an amazing catch, complete with some of the biggest fish any of us had ever seen up close. The struggles we'd had so many times in the past were long in the rear view mirror now and only served to make the triumphs we'd experienced that day all the more sweet.

As the day dipped into the evening and we headed back to the dock, we were treated to a glorious-looking sunset. The captain of the boat made a comment about how he couldn't believe how nice the day had turned out and that he would have been kicking himself if he'd canceled again. We all nodded our assent—the whole experience had been amazing beyond words.

We packed up the car to head home, and a sense of utter peace and quiet fell over the harbor. Dad and I leaned up against a fence while we waited for my son to get out of the bathroom, and looked out at the picturesque pinks, yellows, and purples in the sky. In the stillness of the ever-setting sun, both of us were a little overwhelmed by the sheer magnificence of the day. I looked over at him and there was joy on his face in that moment that spoke volumes—this was a fishing experience he'd wanted his entire life, and now he'd just had it.

Wistfully looking out into the water where we'd just shared an adventure we'd never forget he said, "Today, we have been just been given an incredible gift."

I agreed, but I didn't completely appreciate the magnitude of the gift we'd been given until several months later. We didn't know it at the time, but Dad would be gone just under three months from the date we'd finally been able to make it out; that last fishing trip was the last we would ever go on together, and it was the best one we'd ever had by a wide margin. I have now come to see that the gift we'd received that day was so much more than good fishing and fellowship on the lake—it was a miracle moment of time that created some of the best memories my son and I have of Dad.

Portrait 9

DAD had many passions in his life—family, church, sailing, his work, and a host of other things. If you spent any length of time with him, you'd find all of this out very quickly. Outward expressions of the things he poured his life into were scattered all over our home and his office—pictures, brochures, books, you name it.

Still, there was one passion he had that wasn't as easy to identify by just glancing around. For you to know this one, you had to share a meal with Dad, to talk with him about how he could tell that what he was eating was well-prepared and watch his eyes get big when dessert came. Afterwards, you would realize that not only was food one of his passions, but you would sincerely wonder just how high up it was in the pecking order of things most important to him. Certainly, it wasn't as high up as family and church, but it probably didn't out rank much else!

Looking at Dad, though, you'd never know it—as much as he loved good food, the taste of fine chocolates, and the occasional glass of wine, he was as skinny as a rail his whole life. In fact, with his tall and lanky frame, you would have thought that the man barely ate anything. However, that was anything but the case. He loved a big meal, complete with all the fixings, as much as anyone. It is therefore not too hard to imagine what his favorite holiday was—it was Thanksgiving by a mile.

While Dad wasn't a "champagne and caviar" type of person, he did have this philosophy that if you were going to make something, you had an obligation to make it the right way. He was uncompromising on this, never settling for "second best" when he knew there was something better out there. He refused to eat "just anything."

Nevertheless, it wasn't solely Dad's insistence on quality that I think of when I think about his relationship with food—there was something else to it: his ability to get fixated on a very specific item or dish and talk about it nonstop until he got it. If you have ever had a child who asks when you can have pizza for dinner again, it was kind of like that, only far less annoying and just a touch awkward.

For example, for whatever reason, one of the things that Dad would go on and on about was blueberry muffins. Mom made them fairly often, and he would sample various other offerings from all kinds of local establishments and family friends. As my brother put it, "The man literally lived for the taste of all that flour, sugar, and tart fruit."

There was one particular blueberry muffin, though, that Dad had determined was the best ever. These muffins were a staple on the sailboat that Dad sailed the Port Huron to Mackinac races on, and he asked countless times for the recipe. In fact, Dad was still talking about those muffins while he was in the hospital, just two days before he died.

There were also special events like birthdays or holidays that became an opportunity for Dad to push his "agenda." Whoever was hosting the party was always asked two questions well in advance of the event: "What's for dinner?" and "What's for dessert?" (always in that order). Often, he would be excited by what he heard, but if there was a precise something he was expecting, he'd always ask about it. "Oh," he'd say, "you're not going to be making those twice-baked potatoes like last time? Those are soooooooo good!" This was his not-so-subtle way of letting you know what his preferences were, perhaps for you to either reconsider a certain dish's omission from the menu for the upcoming celebration or to make sure it was included for the next one.

But, just because Dad pushed his favorite foods, that didn't mean he was opposed to trying something new. He most definitely wasn't, though this could get him in trouble from time to time. I remember when we were younger the time that we as a family attended a church potluck. Mom had warned us ahead of time to take it easy with the food, telling us not to eat too much of anything and to stay away from anything remotely questionable. As we went up to go grab some dinner, we remembered Mom's advice, and most of us ended up with "safe" things like bread and salad on our plates.

I say most of us because there was one member of our party who completely ignored Mom's advice—Dad. He had gotten caught up in all of the tantalizing dinner smells and had, as a result, piled heaps of food on his plate. Mom tried to warn him one last time, but Dad was having none of it, digging in with full gusto once he got back to our table.

After Dad had gotten through about half the food on his plate, he paused for a moment to lean over to Mom. "This stuff ain't too bad," he chided, as if to say, "See, everything's fine! You're too paranoid!"

As it turned out, he would never live those words down. Very shortly after dinner, Dad told Mom that he needed to run home because he wasn't feeling well. He disappeared for what seemed like hours while his digestive system violently showed its disapproval of the food he'd eaten. "This stuff ain't too bad" became a life lesson for all of us; when Mom says stay away from something, it is wise to heed her advice. Suffice it to say that we never attended another pot luck after that!

Despite a few bad episodes, however, Dad's mealtime experiences were mostly extremely positive. He always had a big smile on his face at mealtimes, and he was never shy with a compliment to the chef (usually Mom). Dining was an experience he savored and slowed down for, something all too rare in today's extremely over-rushed society.

What Dad couldn't know during all his years enjoying himself at the table was that his developed passion for food would have such a key role in his cancer treatment, helping in prolonging his life far beyond anyone's expectations.

The famous Greek physician Hippocrates once said, "Let food be thy medicine and medicine be thy food," and this was a saying that Dad took completely to heart after receiving his cancer diagnosis. The prognosis was poor—most patients who get the news Dad got don't make it past six months. But, undeterred, he gathered all the research material he could and talked to a couple of doctor friends he knew about what types of foods he should be consuming to maintain his health and give his body the vitamins and minerals it needed in order to have the best chance of fighting the disease off.

He began to consume nothing but organic food, and avoided like the plague anything that was processed, from a box, or in a can. He swore off anything with high fructose corn syrup in it, and started avoiding gluten. His sugar intake was severely restricted (which was tough for a man who made a living in the candy business!). Fast food was a major no-no. Consuming giant salads became a daily occurrence. The changes Dad made were radical and quick, but Dad figured that he had no other choice. Eating his way to better health, rather than just eating for enjoyment and sustenance, became the focus of meal times. And it worked.

As Dad learned more and more and incorporated his new-found knowledge into his diet, he implored the rest of us to do the same so we could live the healthiest lives we could. Dad made it sound like it was our choice, but in some ways, it really wasn't. He was always checking up on all of us to make sure we weren't overdoing it on junk food, buying the right stuff at the grocery store, and making every effort to prepare everything we ate from scratch.

Further, Dad took a very firm stand about never cheating on his new diet whether he was at home or someplace else. So, if we wanted him to come over for breakfast, lunch, or dinner, he made it clear that everything that was served would have to be made with healthy ingredients or he would politely decline, show up but not eat anything, or (more typically) be there but have his own stuff to munch on.

It would have been easy to get offended by his stubborn insistence on never compromising even on one meal, but we all understood his position and why he was doing it. Thus, accommodating Dad's new diet became one of the ways we as a family supported him during the years he spent as a cancer patient. And besides, it wasn't like the stuff he refused to eat was super good for us anyway—when weighed against everything else, it really wasn't all that hard to give it up.

Still, that first year when we were all adjusting to the innumerable changes he made to his eating habits had its ... challenges. It turned out that it wasn't enough to simply avoid certain processed and non-organic foods; there were also ingredients we had to learn to stay away from. For instance, Dad wouldn't eat anything with vegetable oil in it, which we used all the time to sauté just about everything with. So, we'd substitute with olive oil, but it had to be organic and cold pressed. And, he preferred imported varieties from Europe because their olive oil standards are higher than those in the United States. In some ways, it was a cat and mouse game—every time we'd thought we "cracked the code," there would be another wrinkle he'd throw at us.

After a few months of this, I became pretty frustrated about coming up short fairly often, and resolved to make a dessert for Thanksgiving that year that Dad would be completely unable to say no to. I found a recipe for a pecan and coconut pie and heavily modified the recipe so that it didn't contain a thing Dad couldn't eat. The crust was made with organic whole wheat flour and butter. The pecans were organic, soaked in salt water to deactivate the enzyme inhibitors in them, and dried for a day in a food dehydrator so more of their nutrients would be preserved. The coconut was organic, shredded by hand, and toasted myself in our oven so that it didn't have any sweeteners or preservatives in it. The other ingredients needed to make the pie—eggs, buttermilk, vanilla, sugar—were either organic off the shelf or replaced in the recipe with acceptable healthy substitutes.

The ironic thing about making this pie is that the recipe was classified as "easy," but this turned out to be one of the most time consuming baking operations my wife and I had ever undertaken.

I decided to call the treat we'd made "no excuses pie," and when I placed it on the counter when we arrived for the Thanksgiving feast, I placed a big sign on it declaring not only its name, but all the ingredients in it so Dad could see the lengths we'd gone to in order to ensure it was "worthy." Dad smiled when he saw it, and I think it meant a lot to him that we'd put so much effort into making it for him. It also helped that it tasted pretty good too.

As much as Dad relied on dietary changes to help get him into better health, he still had another weapon in his food arsenal…juicing. Shortly after receiving his diagnosis, Dad had some doctor friends who had suggested that starting a regular juicing routine would be incredibly beneficial for him. Before we knew it, Dad had researched all of the different juicers on the market, analyzed them for durability and their effectiveness at extracting maximum juice from raw fruits and vegetables, and difficulty with clean up. It was here that Dad made a difficult choice—the model he liked for juice production was highly recommended by many of the people he talked to, but it wasn't exactly easy to clean up. And by "not easy to clean up" I mean that this juicer was obnoxious. I think it took twice as long to clean up as it did to use it.

Dad bought it anyway, however, and tried to be efficient with it by juicing a few days' worth of juice at a time (he couldn't go much more beyond that, or the juice would go bad). He bought a number of small mason jars for storage and drank the juice right out of them. It was kind of ridiculous looking, but because he did this, I often would jokingly refer to this production as his "little moonshine operation."

The juices he made were … I guess "revolting" is the right terminology for them. These things looked, smelled, and tasted disgusting. The combinations of things he would juice together made my skin crawl—Dad said they were great for fighting cancer, but if there was ever a time to talk about a cure being worse than the disease, I felt that this was it.

For example, one of his juice recipes called for a combination of things like chard, cucumber, kale, spinach, broccoli, parsley, peppers, and a host of other things that had absolutely no business being mixed together. As he learned more and more about juicing and about the things that would bring him the most health benefits, Dad stumbled upon the idea of juicing wheatgrass plants. Because it was expensive, he even starting growing it himself in a little greenhouse he'd bought. Thus, he had trays of wheatgrass in all of its various stages readily on hand, ensuring that he never ran out. However, wheatgrass juice tastes awful—it is literally like trying to drink a freshly cut lawn.

Through it all, even though the juicer was a pain to clean, the results not so tasty, and the fresh organic produce was expensive, Dad was determined and diligently stuck with the program right until he no longer had the strength to do it.

And when I say he "diligently stuck with the program" I mean that Dad, when it came to juicing, he put his entire life on hold to get it done. At times, he even seemed oblivious of what hour of day it was. One time during the summer before he passed away, Dad's brother from out of town was at the house for a visit and spent the night. Despite the fact that his brother was used to getting to bed very late and the fact that it was 6 AM, Dad fired up the juicer and started buzzing the assortment of fruits and vegetables he had in front of him right through that baby as if it were two in the afternoon and he was by himself.

Dad's brother, not surprisingly, was not amused, calling downstairs in a justifiably irritated tone, "Don't you realize you have a GUEST?" When Mom told us that story, all of us laughed but none of us were surprised—that wasn't the first time Dad had done something like that. When he got into his "juicing zone," there was no stopping him.

Eventually, as happens with most cancer patients, Dad started to lose his appetite and hence, his interest in food, as he got closer to the end. It was when that happened that the realization that he would not be with us much longer began to set in. At the same time, though, I also recognized that Dad's passion for food fueled a revolution in all of us with the foods we consume and the choices we make with our health. While he may be gone, he gave us all an incredible gift and the impact of that gift will be with us for the rest of our lives. I know for a fact that Dad was pretty proud of leaving behind that part of his legacy.

Oh, by the way—those blueberry muffins Dad couldn't get enough of? My brother spoke with someone "in the know" about them the day after Dad passed away, and he was informed that the "world's best muffins" were made from a box mix. Who would have guessed it?

I AM AN OPTIMIST. IT DOES NOT SEEM TOO MUCH USE BEING ANYTHING ELSE.

– WINSTON CHURCHILL

Portrait 10

W HEN I started this project, I had no idea that this would be the last portrait of Dad that I would finish. While it might seem odd and a little backwards to have the "ending" of the book finished before all of the middle parts are done, that is not at all a foreign concept to me. I am the type of writer that needs to know where he's going before being able to complete the "stuff in between" with any sense of clarity or focus.

Yet, as I type these words exactly a year to the day (really) since Dad left us, I feel like it's a perfect place for me to conclude the main writing work that began so many months ago. This, on the day of his passing, is a day where I can reflect back at what's transpired over the past year, see where we were just twelve months ago, and look towards the future with an uncanny sense of hope and optimism.

I think Dad is smiling down from Heaven at the irony that I "just happened" to land here today, but I also think he would feel it was entirely appropriate. As much sadness as that day brought us, I believe that he wouldn't want us to dwell on what transpired, but rather to be entirely focused on all of the good things that have been going on in our lives. After all, that's the example he set for all of us.

Dad had amazing positive energy that was highly contagious. When he would greet you, it would be with a firm handshake, a huge smile, and a very enthusiastic, "Hey! How are you doing?" He had a gift for interacting with people and lifting them up. You can't do things like that unless you are a positive person yourself—as the saying goes, "You can't give what you don't have." Dad always made sure he had plenty to give.

Virtually every aspect of Dad's life he used to fuel his optimism. His family was a huge gift to him. Vacations and being out on the water filled his soul. He was always thankful for the job he had that provided for all of our needs. His home, reliable transportation, the church—all things to be overwhelmingly grateful for. And then there was his junk collection...

I realize that you may be thinking two things when you read that last sentence. The first is likely something along the lines of, "That's kind of an odd connection you're making." The second is probably something along the lines of "Well, I guess that would make sense if by 'junk collection' you mean that he had a bunch of things like old toys and other personal memorabilia stored away that he'd collected over the years that meant a lot to him."

I'll address the second thought first. Dad's junk collection was pretty much just that—literally a bunch of rather esoteric things that most people throw away. It was old door handles and sink parts, all kinds of various nuts and bolts, electrical switches and plugs, various plumbing fittings, hinges, shade parts, cabinet hardware, you name it. Dad had chests of drawers full of this stuff, and he delighted in finding the exact part he needed in it whenever an oddball need came up.

He also kept an incredible mental inventory of all of the things he had collected over the years. Often, when he needed a part, he would ask one of us (usually my brother or me) to go looking for something, perfectly describing what the part looked like. Often we'd find it, exactly as Dad had described.

The thought occurred to me, though, that you don't keep a collection of stuff like this around unless you're reasonably certain it will come in handy, and this is the connection I see between Dad's optimism and his collection of "spare parts." Where most people would see just a bunch of junk, Dad saw value, even at times where it wouldn't make sense. I think that trait about him defines the man he was, and was a big reason why he was so relentlessly positive all the time.

To talk to him, you would never know he had a bad day. If you asked how Mom or one of us were doing, he'd answer, "Great! I am just so blessed to have them in my life!" If you asked how business was going, he'd say, "Amazing! I think we're set to have an even better year than last year!" If you asked about things in his spiritual life, he'd respond, "You know, God is so good to me. He is doing so many fantastic things in my life right now." That home improvement project he was working on? Well, how could its progress be anything other than, "Making terrific progress every day. We'll be done real soon!"

And yet, if you were really close to Dad or watched him closely, you would know that there were some very real and serious problems going on his life. Life with four kids, all fairly close in age, certainly was not easy, particularly as we entered our teenager/adult years. While Dad did enjoy his work, there were always financial and managerial pressures that caused him a great deal of stress. His busyness didn't always allow him to connect with God or read the Bible the way I think he would have liked. As for home improvement projects, some of them were massive and could last for months or years before getting completed.

So, the question is ... was Dad simply delusional when he gave such positive answers to questions about the things going on his life? Being somewhat more of a "realist" than Dad was, I have to admit that this was a serious question for me for a long time. Like, say you move into a fairly new house, finish the basement with drywall and carpet, and then the basement springs a leak and ruins everything, aren't you supposed to get really angry and frustrated about that? And what about the repair? Having to dig around the foundation and put in a new sump pump well when you're already taxed to the limit with work and family doesn't sound like a whole lot of fun. Shouldn't you be at least *a little* resentful about the lost time and money?

I think a lot of people (myself included) would have had some choice words to say about a giant hassle like that, but not Dad. He'd talk about how his past experience working for a builder had helped him figure out the problem and solve it. He would express gratitude over the fact that not only did he have a home to live in, but that it had a basement at all. When the project was finally done, he'd often proudly show how all the work he put in would ensure that the issue would never crop up again.

Thus, I gradually came to realize that what I originally thought was delusion was actually determination—determination to be focused at all times on the good instead of the negative. He was so good at it that it came as naturally to him as breathing. And if anyone thought a terminal cancer diagnosis was going to stop him from continuing to be that way, they couldn't have possibly been more wrong.

When Dad got the news, he was obviously shaken up by it, but as the days and weeks passed, he became *more determined than ever* to not only avoid the depression that unfortunately affects so many cancer patients, but to be more positive and full of life than ever. In that goal, he succeeded in spades.

In his family life, Dad poured as much love and affection as he could into all of us. He made sure Mom was taken care of and he worked to make sure he was more available for her. He hugged more tightly and told us he loved us more than he ever had in his entire life. He didn't let a single special moment pass him by with his grandchildren. The relationships he had with his brothers and sisters, as well as the ones with his nieces and nephews, were all strengthened and nurtured like never before.

In his work life, Dad had clients to serve and a business to grow. He traveled all over North America meeting new people and developed innovative products and programs. He helped a number of companies deal with tremendous changes in their organizations. My Mom and brother actually nicknamed his office space "the mountaintop" because of all of the good will and enthusiasm that radiated from his corner of the house.

In his spiritual life, Dad was challenged week in and week out to live the kind of life Christians are called to live. Love more. Judge less. Be radically generous. Serve those in need. Take more risks with prayer. He read loads of spirit-lifting books and was more consistent with his Bible reading. Every day, he worked to grow closer to his Creator so that when his time came to see Him face to face, he could be as ready as possible.

On the homefront, Dad took on some of the biggest and most ambitious home improvement projects he'd ever undertaken in his life. He bought many new tools and tack- led projects he'd never attempted before. He built things strong, above building codes, and to last, so that no one would ever have to worry about things falling apart some- time down the road.

In everything he did, pure joy emanated from him like warmth emanates from the sun. He was a hurricane of op- timism and positivity, and would tire everyone else out be- fore he himself became tired. There were many in his life who simply couldn't believe that he had cancer, and I really don't blame them—with the way he acted, it was incredibly easy to forget that he did.

As his life began to wind down and he entered his final months, however, Dad began to feel worse and worse. Con- stant pain and fatigue began to set in, and he was often sick to his stomach. These were not good signs, but only those closest to him had any idea this was going on; he absolutely refused to complain about any of it to anyone. He wouldn't even complain about it in the journal he kept, which Mom inherited after he passed away.

After she'd had some time to read and process through it after his death, we ended up having a funny conversation around it. She couldn't believe the number of times the phrase "Today is the best I've felt in a long time" appeared in it, and not just because of the optimism conveyed in the pages of his journal. It was because she remembered what had *actually* transpired on many of those days Dad had written about—Dad getting sick, Dad getting bad news, Dad having to go to the doctor for treatment, etc. We both laughed at the juxtaposition of his words and what was going on in reality; you would never have known from reading what he wrote that he was getting worse, not better.

But, there were two things that happened near the end of Dad's life that epitomized his optimism, and why, of all Dad's characteristics, this one is my personal favorite.

The first was a day of sailboat racing that he was involved in less than a month before he entered the hospital for his final days. By this time, Dad was visibly not moving around the way he had been able to in years past, and was regularly dealing with pain. But, he found a way to get back out on the lake and do some competitive sailing with the sail club he and my brother were in. It was intense and fun, as usual, but Dad had a moment where he wasn't being quite as careful as he should have been and the boom of the sail smashed him in the face. Blood from the wound (which still hadn't fully healed by the time of his passing) splattered all over his face, his clothing, and the boat.

Now, a lot of people may have stopped what they were doing, gotten some medical attention, and headed home.

But not Dad. He was a mess, but he had the biggest, sloppi-est, smile you've ever seen on his face. My brother got a picture of it, and it's hilarious—what you see is a man bat-tered and bloodied, but loving what he was doing without a single care in the world. He finished the race, by the way, and got second place. Then he did another one! The idea of "quitting" simply was not in his vocabulary. Don't believe me? Well, here's another story that in a way tops this one...

On the Tuesday that Dad entered the hospital, the doc-tors had told him earlier in the day that his condition was growing so serious that they were going to order hospice care to help Mom out. In the car ride on the way home, Dad told Mom—and I am not making this up—that he planned to be doing a lot of travel in the coming year, and that he thought he should get a new car! Mom, who has an amaz-ing sense of humor, had one of those "I can't believe what I am hearing moments," but managed to simply say, "Let's just see how things go for a while and we'll talk about it."

That's the kind of optimist dad was—looking towards the months ahead when he was essentially told that he had weeks left. What an incredible example for the rest of us to try and strive towards!

Now, looking back on the year we've had since he left us, I think we have all done the best we could to carry on that part of his legacy. Truly, so many wonderful things have happened to the family that to count them would take hours. Mom is taken care of. New grandbabies were born. We all have stable homes and employment that enables us to take care of our needs. The projects that Dad wasn't quite able to get finished before he died are done or are get-ting there.

In short, things are pretty good. Actually no, things are great—and, I think we're set to have an even better year than last year!

"HE WAS A MAN WHO ALWAYS HAD MORE PLANS THAN HOURS IN THE DAY, THOUGH UNLIKE THE REST OF US, HE SEEMED CHRONICALLY UNAWARE OF THIS."

Portrait 11

AMONDAWA

THERE is a tribe of people called the "Amondawa" who live deep in the rainforests of South America. They have no watches or calendars with which to measure the passage of hours and days. If you ask someone from this tribe their age, they will simply give you a blank stare and tell you their name; this is how they keep track of their stages of life instead of using years. Curious about what they did last week? Well, that won't work either —their language doesn't even have the words in it to convey such an idea. The best they can do is speak in the abstract about sequences of events they experienced. In short, you could very much say that this is a group of people who have no concept of time.

I am pretty sure that Dad, were he to visit them, would have had no trouble fitting in.

He was a man who always had more plans than hours in the day, though unlike the rest of us, he seemed chroni-

cally unaware of this. It often got him into trouble, and he
tried all kinds of strategies to deal with it like having a
Franklin Planner (he even listened to all of the how-to
tapes that came with it) and then graduating to using elec-
tronic calendars/task lists once the smartphone craze took
over. Nothing he tried was particularly effective, however,
and not because those products were crummy or because
Dad didn't sincerely try. No, Dad's problems in this area
ran much deeper than that.

I guess a good place to start would be with the fact that
Dad, when he needed to estimate how long it would take to
complete something rarely, if ever, was anywhere close to
being accurate. It was so bad that many of us developed our
own coping mechanisms in order to deal with it. Mine was
that I would simply take whatever number he originally
gave me and multiply it by three. Dad laughed when I told
him this, but the truth is that this method almost always
produced a number close to what ended up being reality.

The reason Dad was usually so far off was because he
had a tendency to give you a timeframe that assumed that
every last detail fell into place perfectly, which never actually happened in practice. While that level of optimism is
admirable, it's not realistic—experience should tell you to
always plan for the worst, but I don't think it was even in
Dad's character or mental processes to think that way.

Other times, his projection was off because he would
simply forget how long it took to do something. Like when
Mom and Dad were moving and I showed up on the day to
discover that Dad hadn't packed much of his stuff up yet.
"It won't take that long," was what he said as Mom and I
started nagging him about it. Well, he was wrong—finish-

ing the move took over twice as long as he'd thought it would, causing my uncle to remark at one point, "Did someone forget to tell him he was moving today?"

And then there were the instances where he dished up a combo platter of being both over-hopeful and not realizing just how much work it really took to get something done...

It was early Saturday morning when my brother, my son, and I walked into the house to a main floor room fully insulated and wired, ready for drywall. I looked around at the magnitude of the task ahead and asked the question I suspected I already knew the answer to. "Dad, what day are you having the guy come over to mud and tape?"

"Monday," was the answer. Like in two days. Of course.

I decided to make a preemptive strike and remind Dad that he only had my son and me for the one day. "Don't even call me tomorrow telling me you need help," I warned. "I have had a long week and need a day to rest. You definitely need to get some help lined up for tomorrow."

"We should be fine," he said. "We've got the whole day, and I can finish up whatever's left myself tomorrow."

"Dad, I really think you should get some help lined up for tomorrow."

"We'll see how far we get," he said.

"As long as you know I am off-limits tomorrow."

"Understood," he answered. "Let's get going. We have a lot of work to do."

Fourteen hours later, we left the house utterly sore and exhausted, with only the ceiling work complete and many walls to go. The job turned out to be a very complicated one. The house had been built in the early 20th century, and as a result, the walls were not exactly straight anymore and the ceiling joists had undergone significant settling. We had to test fit a lot of pieces to get the best compromise between covering the surface of the upper part of the room and getting tight joints.

Further, we had to cut around several pot lights using a technique Dad had never tried before. So, there were a couple of mistakes. If all of that weren't hard enough to deal with, we had one other problem. Back when the house was built, the builders had used a very high quality grade of pine for all of the framing, a much harder grade than the wood used today. Because of this, it was more difficult to drive drywall screws into it, and a lot of screw heads popped off before they made it all the way in. When this is all going on while you're already awkwardly positioned and straining to hold a heavy piece of drywall up ... well, it just makes a job that is already pretty tough all the more challenging and time consuming.

At least the hardest part of the job was done, and I had played my part. Sunday would be a much needed day off for me. There was still a lot to do, but Dad didn't seem too concerned. I told him to make sure he had help for tomorrow, and he said he should be fine, that he would make a few calls but probably wouldn't need someone for too long. I shrugged, knowing that this wasn't my problem anymore, reminded him again that I was unavailable, and told him I'd talk to him next week.

Many of you reading this can probably offer a prediction about what happened next. At around 2 PM the next day, I received a phone call from Dad. "I'm in trouble. I woke up late, and I wasn't able to get any help until way later in the day. I know you said you couldn't help, but is there any way you could?"

"Let me call you back in a minute," I answer, sighing while hanging up.

"That was your Dad, wasn't it?" my wife asks.

"Yeah."

"He needs help doesn't he?"

"Yes, and I even told him specifically that he needed to get other people to help him tomorrow and NOT to call me."

She gives me one of those knowing looks. "Go help your Dad. You know it's the right thing to do. Besides, you have known the man for over thirty years; did you *really* think this wasn't going to happen?"

My wife was right, of course. Dad getting himself in over his head like that was as common as the sun rising every morning. Though he didn't do it on purpose, he was constantly getting bailed out by his kids, his friends, and more often than not, Mom.

Dad was really lucky to have her, and he knew it; she did the best she could to keep him on schedule, remind him of commitments he had, and did whatever she could for him when what needed to get done couldn't fit into the time available. Dad was constantly in motion, but it was thanks to Mom that everything ran as smoothly as it seemed from the outside.

There were some time-related *faux pas*, however, that Mom was powerless to help with. They were those instances where she was not with him and he'd gotten entirely too wrapped up in what he was doing. One occasion that stands out is when he had decided to go for a "quick sail" with my younger sister and our grandmother, and they ended up being gone for several hours. It's not hard to envision that some amount of concern would start to set in at that point. Shouldn't they have made it back by now?

Imagine Mom's reaction, then, when Dad finally called her from a pay phone to tell her that they were currently at a harbor fifteen miles up the lake from where they'd started. Being that far "off course" is honestly a pretty difficult mistake to make, but Dad made it all the same. They had apparently been thoroughly enjoying the sun and the waves, and he just wasn't paying attention to how far they'd traveled and how long they'd been out there.

Stuff like this happened in all sorts of places and circumstances—at home, at friend's houses, at special events, at the office, etc. Thankfully, cellphones were eventually invented and became portable enough to always have available in one's pocket. This at least helped locate Dad when he'd "run over" again, but they were absolutely useless with curbing the behavior in the first place.

Dad made up for all of it, though, by always being there for you when you needed him, regardless of what he had going on. He was always "available" (even when he really wasn't) and would treat you like you were a VIP whenever he was with you. The most precious gift Dad could give you was his time, and he gave it freely to anyone who asked. He might show up anywhere from fifteen to sixty minutes after he'd said he would, but his word was his bond—if he said he'd be there, there was literally nothing that was going to keep him from delivering on his promise.

I think it's fair to say, though, that Dad's relationship with the hour, minute, and second hand was a complicated one. He was never in a hurry despite constantly being over booked. He would often start new projects when he had multiple unfinished ones queued up. He was a visionary but not a planner. He would help anyone who asked for it, but rarely recognized when he needed it himself.

For all of Dad's life, he got away with being able to manage his time like that. It should therefore come as no surprise, then, that as he neared the end of his days with us, Dad seemed to be completely oblivious to something that was painfully obvious to the rest of us—the man who never seemed to run out of time was quickly running out of it. Luckily, though, Dad got a much-needed intervention at just the right moment.

It started with a conversation I had with him the Sunday before he passed away. My family and I saw him at church, and he was clearly feeling quite uncomfortable by that point. Trying to distract him a little bit, I happened to ask him how my brother was doing, and how plans to have him take over more of the day-to-day operations of his business were going.

Dad told me things were going pretty well, relating the different ways they had been working together over the past several months. But, at present, my brother was in the middle of a major renovation project on his house in order to make enough room for the new baby he and his wife had on the way. It was a lot of hard work and extremely late nights, he said, so Dad didn't feel that now was the right time to push "business stuff" too hard.

I agreed with him in principle on his approach, but I'd be lying if I said there wasn't some amount of cognitive dissonance between what I was agreeing with and the man before me whose condition was clearly deteriorating. After telling Dad I'd talk to him later, this continued to gnaw at my thoughts. How much longer did he think he could afford to keep putting stuff like that on hold?

This question was still on my mind as I drove to work the next day. Because of a construction project along my normal path to the office, I ended up taking an alternate route that was going to go right by Dad's house. As I got closer, I had an overwhelming feeling that I needed to stop and see him before going into work. I called him to make sure he was home, and arrived minutes later.

Dad was up in his office, wearing the most comfortable clothes he had, looking worse than I'd seen him the day before. "Dad," I explained, "I really think you need to re-think some of the things you've got going and focus on your health and making sure you're fully prepared for what might happen next."

I expected him to resist, but to my surprise, he agreed without a fight. After a few more minutes of discussion, he called my brother over to talk, and we gave him the short version of what Dad and I had been talking through. After we had filled him in, we strategized around what was going on and what the priorities needed to be for everyone.

There was obviously stuff with his business, but there were also things with the houses and Mom that Dad needed to be sure were taken care of too. It didn't take long for a plan to come together, and as we wrapped up and got ready to set it in motion, Dad glanced at both of us, told us how proud he was, and thanked us for being sons he could count on.

It was my brother who seemed to sense what Dad was really saying through the words that he'd just spoken. "JP," he said, "we've got this. You have set up everything perfectly and all we have to do is follow your lead. You don't need to worry about a thing—everything is taken care of and that won't stop no matter what happens to you."

I believe Dad knew this intellectually, but there was clearly power in those words for him in that moment. They validated the countless instances where we had supported him over the years, and that he could move forward with assurance that he would have all of the help he needed for whatever remaining days he had.

It turned out to be extremely fortunate that we'd had that conversation. The day we'd all circled up in Dad's office turned out to be the last time I saw Dad when he wasn't heavily medicated by pain relievers. Looking back on it, I feel like there was more to it than me having such a "strong urge" to stop in that morning. I believe that God still has a voice, that He knew more about Dad's condition than any of us, and that when He saw that Dad needed a push, He used an unexpected detour to provide one.

The next several days were a blur of activity, but it was really awesome to see the truth my brother had spoken affirmed time and again throughout the five or so days Dad spent in the hospital—not just by the two of us, but by family and friends who lent their time and talents to pitch in and help out.

Typically, Dad hadn't planned his last days out perfectly, but he had the love and support of those around him to ensure that it would all turn out OK, just as we'd always had.

"MOM'S LIVING ROOM WAS PRACTICALLY AGLOW AS WE FONDLY RECALLED ALL THE THINGS WE DID TOGETHER AND WHAT HE MEANT TO ALL OF US AS INDIVIDUALS."

Portrait 12

I N the morning on Sunday, October 19th, 2014, Mom woke up at her usual time of 5 AM thinking that today might be the day that Dad would finally be at peace. Saturday had been pretty rough for him, and he was now in a state where he was sleeping nearly all the time. My younger sister, who is a nurse and had seen countless patients in the state Dad was now in, didn't think it would be too much longer.

My wife, kids, and I went to church that day, and then went to get pumpkins, apple butter, cider, and donuts afterwards at a local cider mill near our home. The day was warm and beautiful, and taking an hour or two to enjoy some tastes of fall seemed like a good way to take our minds off things for a while. And, while we there, I recalled fondly the many times Mom and Dad had taken us to the cider mill after church on Sundays when we were kids.

As the day wore on into the evening, a kind of stress set in that was difficult to describe that I can only imagine was several orders of magnitude worse for Mom. I think we had all accepted that Dad was not going to make it, but the question for all of us was, "How long would he be stuck in limbo literally waiting for his body to give out?" We knew he wasn't in any pain thanks to the medications the doctors had him on, but I couldn't help thinking over and over that this was no way to live. And, I don't think I was alone in thinking this; we just wanted it to be over, for his sake.

Being on pins and needles the whole day, jumping at every phone call and text message waiting for news created this unsettled state of mind that made it difficult to think about much else or plan anything. About the only thing I could do was take a walk to get some fresh air and try and clear my head. Not really wanting to be alone, I asked my wife to go with me.

The topic of conversation was about what you'd expect, but at least I had someone there to try and process through all of it with. We talked about what the doctors felt about Dad's condition, how Mom was holding up through all of this, and what the most likely timing was going to be for the visitation and funeral so we could start making plans for her job and the kids' school schedule.

At one point in the conversation my wife stopped and said, "This is all so sudden and so hard. I don't really want to think about any of this anymore. I just want to hear about good news, like babies being born."

Right after she said that, she pulled out her phone to see what was going on with her social media circles in order to provide a needed distraction from the heaviness of what was transpiring. To my surprise, she started laughing. Relieved but a little confused, I asked what was going on. She didn't say a word, but showed me what was on her tiny screen. The first several posts in her feed were all pictures of new babies. I smiled at her and said, "Honey, I think God just answered a prayer for you."

We returned home and as we all prepared to go to school/work the next day, I received a text message from my brother. Dad had just died, peacefully, not in pain and in his sleep. It was all finally over.

Mom, who had been with him the whole day, headed home to get some rest. My wife and I circled up our kids to process the news as a family. We gave each other hugs and said a few prayers for the family, and tried to get some sleep ourselves. Tomorrow and the next few days were going to be very busy as we started to plan the remembrance and celebration of Dad's life.

Mom and my aunt handled most of the visitation arrangements with the funeral home, and she asked me to see what I could do as far as coordinating the memorial service. Our long-time friend who was the pastor of the church Dad and my family attended was honored to be asked to officiate the memorial proceedings. But, since the church was portable and didn't yet have a building, we needed to find a place for the service to be held.

The most obvious course of action was to use the chapel attached to the church our pastor had come from and still had connections with, but it was going to be difficult for us to get it for the date/time we wanted. Luckily, even though Dad was gone, he had a solution for us in his

contact list—the cell phone number of one of the lead pastors at the church we'd been trying to book the chapel at.
He and Dad had been very good friends for years.

I called and got his voicemail. I left a message for him,
telling him the news about Dad, and asking if there was a
way he could help us get the situation with the service set-
tled. I expected to hear back from him in a few hours or
maybe the next day, but he literally called me a few minutes
later. We shared a few fond memories of Dad, and he
promised to make sure the chapel matter was taken care of.
"After all of the times your Dad helped me out," he said,
"this is the least I feel I could do for his family."

As it turned out, we had one other ask for him. Because of the relationship he had with Dad, would he be willing to share a some thoughts about him at his memorial? It
turned out he was free and more than willing. With two
terrific pastors who knew Dad so well lined up to speak at
the service, we knew that the day was going to a great trib-
ute to his memory.

I relayed the good news to Mom and she asked me to
take care of one more thing for her. She wanted to have
someone playing music at a couple of points during the
service. It turned out that was easy enough to arrange, but
we had to decide what he was going to play and when the
music would come in during the service. Looking for inspi-
ration, Mom asked for some of the songs that we sang in
church that had meant something to Dad. There were
many to choose from, but there were four in particular that
jumped out at us during the search, and once chosen, the
times when they should be played became obvious.

In the next few paragraphs as I discuss each song we selected, I encourage you to pause for a few moments and take a listen to them before continuing on with the narrative. I think that by doing so that you will get a strong sense of how these songs became such an important part of how we ultimately wanted to honor and remember Dad.

The first selection we chose was "Great I Am" by Phillips, Craig, and Dean, and this is the song we opted to begin the memorial with.

The lyrics of the song are about a person whose strongest desire is to be close to God, and in listening to it, it was hard not to think about Dad. The words perfectly reflected his heart towards his Creator, and were a reminder to everyone in the room of the reality of the promise of Heaven. We felt that starting the proceedings off this way gave everyone a set of lenses with which to view everything that would come after; that though we would be grieving as a family, we could be comforted by the fact that Dad was now in a place where he could live the words of the song out in every moment, and that truth was good news indeed.

After that, our pastor would convey some thoughts to us about how God was not the author of Dad's cancer, encourage us to mourn with hope because of Dad's relationship with Jesus Christ, and share a few family memories. When he was done, the next song would be "How He Loves" by John Mark McMillan.

This song uses vivid and striking imagery to describe the beautiful, unconditional, and unfathomable love our Father has for us. The chorus of the song is amazing, repeating slight variations of the phrase "He loves us" over and over again. When you hear the words repeated so many times, you start to feel not only a powerful sense of the way God loves Dad as one of His precious children, but also the love Dad had for his family and his friends. For me, it meant that I had two great and loving Fathers in Heaven always watching over me.

At that point, the pastor who had helped us get the chapel reserved would share a few words about Dad, his faith, and the gift he was to all who knew him. Then, "10,000 Reasons" by Jonas Myrin and Matt Redman would be played.

The song is loosely based on Psalm 103, a psalm of David where his heart is singing about the goodness of God and what He does for His people. Near the end of the song, the lyrics transition to a person who is near the end of their life, yet still finds a way to keep on praising God as their life fades away. Those words could not have epitomized Dad's last days in the hospital any better.

The service would conclude with "Light Up the Sky" by The Afters.

The song addresses people who feel alone and are struggling with hope, feelings that would no doubt be entering the thoughts of many of those present at the memorial as it wrapped up. They would need something concrete to hang onto, and the chorus of the song contains a magnificent promise that I think we would all need to hear as we all prepared to say goodbye to Dad for the last time. Despite our grieving hearts, God's presence would be thick amongst us, so obvious that it would be impossible for any of us to miss it.

And truly, as we entered into the days ahead, it was. Mom, my aunt, my sisters, and a few others had done a beautiful job with the flowers and putting together picture boards of some great snapshots in time of Dad's life. The visitation was packed with people Dad knew, each with their own stories and remembrances they were all too glad to share. There were handshakes and hugs, tears of sorrow, all with plenty of moments of levity mixed in. Though he never wanted to make a big deal over himself, I think Dad would have been pleased and humbled by the way the whole afternoon/night honored his life.

There was also the evening Mom, some of her siblings, and my brother and sisters spent with the officiating pastor talking over the special family moments that would be shared during the service. There were so many fantastic memories and character traits we all shared about Dad; Mom's living room was practically aglow as we fondly recalled all the things we did together and what he meant to all of us as individuals. We laughed—a lot—about some of the crazy things Dad did and our favorite moments with him. I even learned a few things that I never knew happened.

My favorite of those stories was one my older sister shared regarding her wedding day. As she was preparing to be escorted down the aisle by Dad, he decided that right then would be a good time to take a "potty break." When the wedding coordinator gave the cue to start heading down to the front of the church, Dad wasn't back yet. When my sister didn't move and started gesturing back, the fear was she'd gotten cold feet. But, that obviously wasn't it; they just needed to wait for Dad to finish washing his hands.

As funny as that was, Dad wasn't done with his antics before giving his first-born daughter away. On their way to the altar, he decided to pause and thank one of his business partners for coming to the ceremony. Harmless, sure, but perhaps not the best time to do that, especially after the commotion he'd caused in the back of the church already! Yet, that was so Dad; when he got an idea in his head, he simply couldn't help but see it through.

As we were getting ready to leave our little gathering that evening, Mom shared one last story with all of us that touched my heart. It was a well-known fact that Mom got up very early every morning and that she liked to start getting ready for bed at 9:30 PM. Dad, however, had this way of forgetting about this virtually every single night. When Mom would call him to bed, he never ceased to give her a look that said, "This is news to me. Why didn't you say something earlier?" It's the type of thing that would be maddening if it also weren't so sincere.

But, on his last day with us, it seems that Dad finally remembered. When he passed away, Mom looked over at the clock. It was 9:32 PM. As he lay there asleep and fading away, he had still managed to give her one last gift.

Afterword

"The last few days have been some of the most challenging of my life. I am sitting here with Tom recounting some of life's great joys. While challenging, they have also been the most BLESSED, as we've talked about some of the deep things in our lives..."

-Dad's last journal entry, October 16, 2014

DAD is way more alert today than he was yesterday —he is still stuck in the hospital bed dealing with major pain issues, but he acting way closer to his normal self than the "in and out of it" person I saw yesterday. The improvement in his condition gives me a small hope that maybe this isn't quite the end yet, even though we all sense that it's days, maybe up to a week, away.

Perhaps most encouraging is that Dad, who had been fighting nausea and simply hadn't been able to eat much since he'd been taken to the emergency room, told me that he was very hungry and wanted to eat something that wasn't cafeteria food. He asked if I would go get him "the healthiest thing on the menu" from Panera Bread, and I soon returned with a turkey-avocado sandwich and a bowl of tomato soup for him.

I didn't really expect him to be able to eat it all, but he wolfed everything I brought him down in just a few minutes. I actually worried that he'd eaten so fast that he wouldn't be able to keep it down, but he didn't seem to be having any problems at all. In fact, I could see strength and color returning to his face with every bite he took.

As he ate, we talked about how he was doing and about some business things my brother was in the process of handling, but our conversation soon turned to a book our pastor had recommended to us called *Kisses from a Good God* by Paul Manwaring. The story is autobiographical, and details Paul's journey from receiving a prostate cancer diagnosis to being fully restored to health. The book's emphasis is on how God had poured blessing after blessing on him to keep him going during that very dark time in his life, calling each lift in his spirits a "kiss" from God.

Dad had started reading the book, but he hadn't gotten a chance to finish it. I had, however, and was immediately struck by many of the core similarities between Dad's story and Paul's. There were, of course, differences, but there was one truth both Dad and I knew—that God had "kissed" his life the way He had Paul's, perhaps even more so.

On impulse, I made Dad start to list out all of the wonderful things he'd experienced over the years since his diagnosis. He not surprisingly started with family, talking about how lucky he was to have Mom and his kids, and the many ways his grandchildren were a blessing to him. He expressed excitement about the new babies that were on the way, knowing full well the joy both would bring with their arrival. He recollected some of his fonder memories and mishaps with all of us, smiling and laughing over all of the different moments.

He talked about the business he'd started and all of the wonderful people he'd had the privilege of working with over the years. He was grateful that he'd had the opportunity to build a company that both provided income and allowed him to deliver great products that people loved. He also knew that what he'd worked so hard to build would continue because he had left it in the best possible of hands.

A lot of cancer patients spend days and sick and weak from chemotherapy treatments, yet when you looked at Dad, you would never have known there was anything wrong with him until his last few weeks. Dad was very proud of the fact that he'd lived four years beyond his original prognosis, and that until two days ago, he hadn't been hospitalized at all because of cancer. He was pleased that everyone in the family was following his lead and taking eating right and wellness seriously. He was thankful for all of the care the doctors and nurses had given him.

Dad reflected back on the summer and saw all the times he not only got a chance to go out sailing, but the number of times he'd done well when he was out racing with his friends. He recalled the day he, my uncle, my son, and I had spent fishing and all the fun we'd had.

Most of all, though, Dad was relieved to know that Mom would be taken care of, not just financially, but that she had an army of friends and family close by who would always be there for her.

Dad went on for close to an hour about all of the "kisses" in his life, and he knew that there were way too many of them for it all to have been some big accident. Once you started listing everything out, it was impossible to not realize that our good, good Father was watching over Dad this whole time.

When Dad was done, there was a pause as I happened to look out the lone window in the room Dad was currently a patient in. It was a gorgeous fall day outside, with the sun shining and the nearby trees in the prime of their autumn splendor. As I gazed upon the outside world, considering for a moment all that Dad had just said, a thought came to me.

"Dad, come here and look out this window."

Dad got out of the bed and carefully made his way over. I stood next to him and asked, "Do you see the trees? The reds, the yellows, the browns, and the oranges?"

"Yes," he answered.

"Dad, the leaves on those trees are dying, but God has made it all look beautiful. And, that's what he's done for you, for your life."

Dad's eyes welled up a little as understanding washed over him. He looked at me and just nodded, overwhelmed by the sheer magnitude of the kisses that had been poured on *his* life by a very good God.

CPSIA information can be obtained
at www.ICGtesting.com
Printed in the USA
BVHW032032100619
550631BV00001B/1/P

9 781943 866038